D0625809

**Affordable Alternatives
to Service Stations**

NEAR THE
MOTORWAYS

(8th Edition)

**by
Hugh Cantlie**

Over 200 pubs, inns, hostelries and
places of interest just 5 minutes off
a motorway junction.

Co-author of
5 Minutes off the Motorway

Published by Cheviot Books

1st Edition	Sep 2001	Reprint	Jan 2002
2nd Edition	Sep 2002	3rd Edition	Oct 2003
4th Edition	Oct 2004	5th Edition	Jan 2006
6th Edition	Feb 2007	7th Edition	Feb 2008
8th Edition	Apr 2010		

| Copyright | Hugh Cantlie |
| Illustrations | Hugh Cantlie |

The contents of this book are believed correct at the time of printing. Nevertheless, the publisher cannot be held responsible for any changes in the details given in this guide, nor for the consequences of any reliance on the information provided by it.

All rights reserved. No part of this publication may be re-produced, stored in any retrieval system, or transmitted in any form or by any other means, electronical or me-chanical, including photocopying and recording or by any information storage retrieval system - unless the written consent of the publisher has been obtained be-forehand.

This book may not be sold, resold, hired out or other-wise disposed of by way of trade in any form of binding or cover other than that in which it is published, without the prior consent of the publisher.

A catalogue copy is held by the British Library.

Cheviot Books
Mill Cottage, Stourton, Warwickshire CV36 5JA
e-mail: info@cheviotbooks.co.uk
website: www.cheviotbooks.com

ISBN 978-09539920-7-2

Printed by Potts Printers Ltd, Cramlington

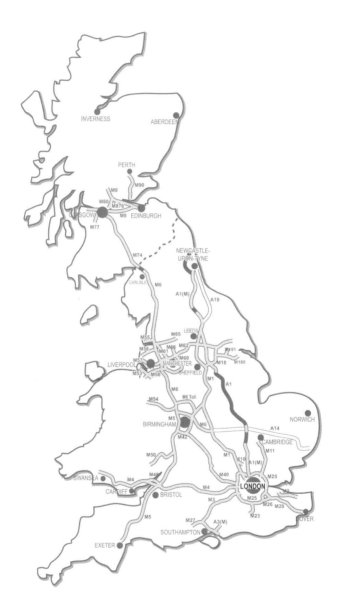

Foreword

Dear fellow motorists,

The last two years have been eventful economically for all of us and accident prone for me. The first mishap occurred when I was walking along a pavement in London and was knocked unconscious by a reversing van. That was four days before I had to start correcting the draft of the previous edition of the guide so I make no apologies if the odd error crept in.

As a result it was decided that I should move south from Northumberland in case of any further problems. So now I am in Warwickshire within easy reach of Banbury station in a rented mill cottage on the River Stour which duly flooded two weeks after arrival.

Last June I had to have an operation on my back at the John Radcliffe as I could hardly walk. I was told that this was apparently nothing to do with my accident but I am glad to say that it was a complete success.

The legal profession are still dealing with the matter but I would counsel caution about the no win, no fee solution.

As a result of all this, the publication of the new edition of the guide was deferred by a year. I have taken the opportunity however to rethink the type of entry in the book due to the ongoing financial recession. I have also decided to cheer things up by having the illustrations in full colour.

Please keep on sending us your comments and experiences. I propose that any such amendments will be published on www.cheviotbooks.com as they occur so that we can all keep up to date.

May we all survive in one way or the other until next year.

Hugh Cantlie

Contents

Motorways, maps and descriptions
The motorways are in numerical order with a separate section for Scotland. Each map is orientated with north at the top but the scale may vary. The longer motorways have been divided up into sections.

Each motorway has a map showing where it is located. Then there is a description of the motorway or section of the motorway with a map showing the junctions. Only those with places off them are shown with the appropriate junction numbers, whilst the others are in grey. This may help you work out the distances involved between likely stops.

A-Roads
The dual carriageway sections of the A1, as well as the A14 and A19, are also included, but are shown in grey as they are not motorways as such.

Page Layout
The blue panel at the top shows the junction number with the towns and road numbers as given on the actual motorway signs. Underneath is a short description you may find of any difficulties (from personal experience) together with a plan showing the location of the entries by a letter(ie A in a roundel) which corresponds with their entry below. Any filling stations are shown by a symbol.

Description of the entry
The name of the entry is given with the corresponding letter in the roundel above. Then the address and the highlighted postcode for SatNav. Below is the telephone number and the website (if applicable) so that you can check on any further details yourself or book a table. Times for the last orders for food, as opposed to drinks, are given, but these can change.

The symbols given below show the number of bedrooms (if applicable) whether coffee or tea is available for passing motorists, facilities for the disabled, outside seating and if dogs and children are welcome. The Pound sign gives the price range. Three being the most expensive.

There is a brief description of each entry to give the feeling of the place and the general welcome. Lastly there is a pen and wash drawing for easier recognition.

Symbols

⬜	Restaurant (for Places of Interest)
14	Number of Bedrooms
☕	Coffee or tea
♿	Disabled
🪑	Outside seating
👫	Children
🐾	Dogs
£-£££	Price range
★	New Entry
⛽	Filling Station

Places of Interest

These are given in a separate panel below the junction plan. Thus Weston Park, built in 1761 and owned by a member of the Historic Houses Association (HHA), which is four miles from the junction and has a café and a restaurant would be shown as:

Weston Park (1671) HHA – 4 miles ☕ ⬜

Ownership is shown by initials:

EH	English Heritage
HHA	Historic Houses Association
HS	Historic Scotland
NT	National Trust
NTS	National Trust for Scotland
Pte	Privately owned

Houses belonging to members of the Historic Houses Association (HHA) are private property but are mostly open to the public. They should be contacted beforehand. Privately owned houses are obviously private but some do open to the public from time to time. A list of all such properties are given on pages 289 - 291 giving details and contact numbers.

Acknowledgements

Every year I say "Never again". So why again? I suppose I must thank the snow we had in January as I was unable to drive anywhere and decided to keep myself busy. Quite how busy that was to prove would probably have deterred me from starting but that applies to anything.

I have been very fortunate in having help for all the information gathered over the past two years as publishing a guide book is a continuous process of squirreling away information for future use. Many of you have made suggestions but Tim O'Connor-Fenton comes in for special mention for his role in checking on the A1 and A19.

The owners, tenants and landlords of all the entries were courteous and helpful answering my questions even though they were trying to serve their customers at the same time.

As usual there have been many people who have helped in the process but my particular thanks are due to Mary Manville-Hales who bravely said that she would help with the typing.

Rollo de Walden however made the whole thing happen as he was responsible for transposing all the typewritten pages into Quark Express and for hours of hard graft, correcting, reshaping and coping with my changes of mind. This was all due to a chance meeting with his parents at an exhibition at Compton Verney, so who says that luck or coincidence does not play a role in all our lives.

There was a hiccup with the production of the maps and plans but Anthony Duke took over and without him we would all have been lost figuratively speaking whilst my brother Paul and Kevin Shearer helped fill some of the gaps.

My thanks are also due to Potts Printers Ltd of Cramlington who printed the previous edition and undertook to do it yet again.

With the current economic climate I have taken out over seventy entries but replaced them with ones to reflect these challenging times. A number of you have contributed to these and we fellow motorists are duly grateful to you.

On my moving to Warwickshire from Northumberland, Tim O'Connor-Fenton has been acting on my behalf by keeping a beady lookout for suitable places in the North East which gives me an excuse to come back to the north to do an unnecessary check.

New entries:

A1	Piccolino	Tim O'Connor-Fenton
	Bowes Incline	Chris Mitchinson
A14	Overstones	Peter Bracher
A19	Carpenters Arms	Tim O'Connor-Fenton
A19	Three Tuns	Tim O'Connor-Fenton
A19	Bay Horse	Tim O'Connor-Fenton
M1	Famous Shoulder	Mrs J.Sweeting
M4	Bird in Hand	Christine Dinan
M5	Nobody Inn	William Maybury
M6	George Hotel	Michael Bowman-Vaughan
M6	Highland Drove	Michael Bowman-Vaughan
M40	Sir Charles Napier	John Carpenter
M48	Afon Gwy Hotel	Toni Spowers
M54	David Austin Roses	Simon Kenyon-Slaney
M56	Honey Bee	Mr R.A.Barker
M65	Thatch & Thistle	Ashley Holt

A1(M)

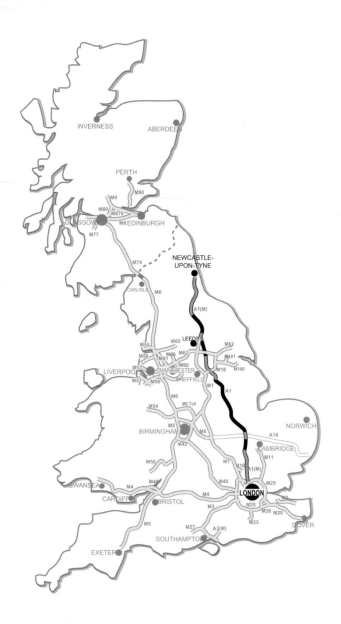

A1(M) London to Newcastle

JUNCTIONS 6 TO 65

The A1 is the old Great North Road from London to Edinburgh and for much of its length it still uses the routes of the old Roman roads.

Due to the increase in traffic on the M1, it is slowly being upgraded to motorway standards especially to the northern sections

Over the past few years it has been upgraded from the junction with the M62 at Ferrybridge to the junction with the A19 north of Boroughbridge.

Work has now started to the section north of Boroughbridge to Leeming which is due to be finished in 2012.

It was planned to continue from Leeming to Scotch Corner to be finished in 2014 but this has been shelved for the time being due to lack of funding.

As a result of these continuing road works I have decided to include the A19 to the Tyne Tunnel as a dual-carriageway alternative to the A1 as far as Newcastle. The A19 does not have numbered junctions.

There are stretches of dual-carriageway still to be upgraded such as from Baldock to Huntingdon and the long section from Peterborough to south of Doncaster. These have been included although the turn-offs are not numbered and only have names of the villages or towns.

For ease of use I have divided the A1 into five different sections. The first is from Hatfield to the junction with the A14 at Huntingdon; the second from Huntingdon to Grantham; the next is from Grantham to the M62 at Ferrybridge and then the section to Scotch Corner. The last is the motorway to Newcastle.

JUNCTIONS 6 TO 13/14

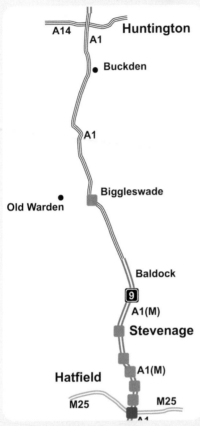

From the junction with the M25 at South Mimms it is a motorway until north of Baldock. Hatfield is bypassed by going underneath it through a tunnel.

Welwyn Garden City was the first of the conceptual towns to be designed to bring the country to the town in the 1920s. It is still a surprisingly pleasant town to live in.

Stevenage was the first of the post-Second World War new towns. Apparently the brother of the Minister responsible for the concept had happened to have bought some of the farms surrounding Stevenage shortly before the details of the intended new town had been published.

Knebworth House, the home of the Lytton family since 1490, is to the west of the motorway by Stevenage.

The A1 continues as a well-maintained dual carriageway north of Baldock until it becomes a motorway again for a short stretch after crossing over the A14 at Huntingdon.

After coming off the Motorway, take the first left on a modern road layout signposted Willian. Head for the church in the centre of the village and the Fox is facing it.

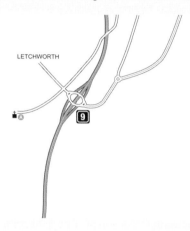

LETCHWORTH

🅐 The Fox at Willian ★

Satnav
SG6 2AE

Baldock Lane, Willian, Herts.
01462 480 233
www.foxatwillian.co.uk

Last orders for food: Weekdays: 2.00pm and 9.15pm. Sundays: 2.45 pm, no evening meals.

££

A restaurant-cum-pub which has been refurbished so is now bare floors with wooden tables. Clean, bright and airy with a cheerful and friendly staff.

By Biggleswade there is a roundabout by a supermarket. Take the B658 marked Old Warden and brown signed for the Shuttleworth Collection. Straight on at the first roundabout and pass the Shuttleworth Collection and Swiss Garden on the left. The Hare and Hounds is 3.5 miles further on to your left as you come into the village of Old Warden.

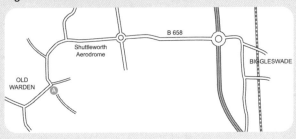

Places of interest

Shuttleworth Collection of Historic Aircraft.

 The Hare and Hounds Satnav **SG18 9HQ**

Main Street, Old Warden, Beds.
01767 627 225
www.hare&houndsoldwarden.co.uk

Last orders for food: Weekdays: 2.00pm and 9.30pm. Sundays: 3.00pm. Closed Mondays.

 ££

A privately owned, comfortable wayside pub cum restaurant which specialises in local game from the nearby Shuttleworth estate as well as Scottish beef. There are three separate dining rooms served by attentive and friendly staff. Just the place if you have left London rather later than planned.

Buckden is just off the A1 – by a Shell garage on a roundabout on its southern edge. As an alternative, the George Hotel and Brasserie is opposite.

The Lion Hotel

Satnav
PE19 5XA

High Street, Buckden, Cambs..
01480 810 313

Last orders for food: Weekdays: 2.00pm and 9.30pm. Sundays: 2.00pm and 9.00pm.

£££

It was built in 1492 as a guest house for the new Bishop of Lincoln's Palace next door. The fireplace and the five spokes of a unique oak ceiling meeting a central boss still remain. Extended in Georgian times, it was converted into a hotel and is an example of a bygone age with personal service and a homely feeling. Bar meals are also available.

JUNCTIONS **13/14** TO GRANTHAM

The first stretch is a four lane motorway until Peterborough, which encourages motorists to forget how heavy their right feet are until it is too late to avoid the cameras. Stamford is a remarkable town for being in a time warp and should be congratulated for turning down the central government offer of a grant to have hanging baskets, street markets and no parking. The George Hotel is world famous as a hostelry. Grantham is now famous for yet another example of government but no marks for guessing who this could be.

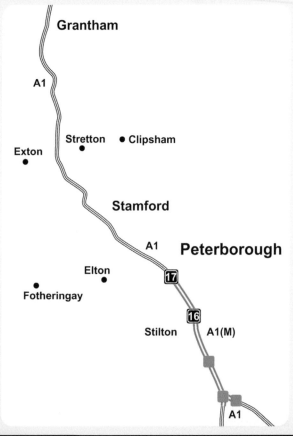

Take the B1043 south and almost immediately, bear right to Stilton.

 Bell Inn Hotel

Great North Road, Stilton, Cambs.
01733 241 066
www.thebellstilton.co.uk

Satnav
PE7 3RA

Last orders for food: Weekdays: 2.00pm and 9.30pm. Sundays: 2.00pm and 9.00pm.

£££

A 16th century coaching inn and now a privately owned well furnished hotel with two bars and a restaurant on two levels under beamed ceilings. There is outside seating in an enclosed garden and private parking. Dick Turpin's room where he rested between nefarious operations is still in use as the resident's lounge. Those looking for Stilton Cheese, which is actually made in Melton Mowbray could be disappointed.

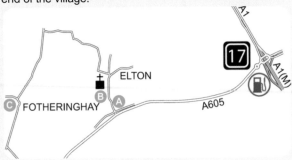

A1(M) **17** Peterborough, Wisbech (A1139)
N'hampton, Oundle A605

Take the A605 to Oundle. After 4 miles turn right signed
Elton. The Loch Fyne Restaurant is about 100 yards on
the right from the turning. Pass the house and grounds of
Elton Hall and the Black Bull is on the left before the
church. You can reach The Falcon by taking a left at the
end of the village.

Places of interest

Elton Hall and Garden (15th & 17thC) H.H.A. 3m

Ⓐ **Loch Fyne Restaurant**

Satnav
PE8 6SH

The Old Dairy, Elton, Northants.
01832 280 298
www.lochfyne.com

Last orders for food: Weekdays: 9.00am to
9.00pm. Saturdays: 9.00am to 9.30pm.
Sundays: 10.00am to 9.00pm

£££

Those of us who have driven along Loch Fyne in Argyll-
shire will have stopped at
John Noble's Loch Fyne
Oyster Bar. This maintains
the same standard and indi-
viduality and the seafood still
comes from Loch Fyne. A
good place to have a kipper
for breakfast on your way
north. Children are permitted,
but dogs outside.

ⓑ The Black Horse

Overend, Elton, Northants.
01832 280 240

Satnav
PE8 6RU

Last orders for food: 2.15pm and 9.00pm.
Sundays: Noon to 7.00pm.

£

A friendly, cheerful village pub with a separate restaurant. A large garden next to the churchyard for summer evenings. A car park is on the other side of the road.

ⓒ The Falcon

Main Street, Fortheringay, Northants.
01832 226 254
www.huntsbridge.com

Satnav
PE8 5HZ

Last orders for food: 2.15pm and 9.00pm.
Sundays: Noon to 7.00pm.

££

An 18th century stone built inn in this attractive village with a garden looking out on to the church. It is full of character and is run with efficiency and personality. There is a locals' bar and a smart dining room as well as a conservatory. Serving a modern British menu.

The Jackson Stops is signed from the road in Stretton.
For the Olive Branch, continue to Clipsham and it is on
the left by a sharp bend. For The Fox and Hounds take
the B668. After Greetham turn left and first left for Exton.
The Fox and Hounds is on the village green.

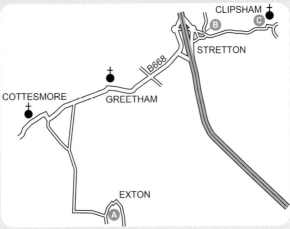

The Fox and Hounds

Satnav
LE35 8AP

The Green, Exton, Rutland
01572 812 403
www.foxandhoundsrutland.co.uk

Last orders for food: Weekdays: 2.00pm and
9.00pm. Sundays: 2.00pm. Mondays: Closed

££

An early 17th century building which was a coaching
inn. It therefore has well-pro-
portioned rooms, one being
the dining room and the other
the bar. Family owned and
run with a special emphasis
on Italian cooking. Friendly
service.

ⓑ Jackson Stops

Rookery Road, Stretton, Rutland
01780 410 237

Satnav
LE15 7RA

Last orders for food: Weekdays: 2.15pm and 9.15pm. Sundays: 2.30pm. No evening meals. Mondays: Bar meals only.

££

This privately owned pub cum restaurant has changed hands and now has a good standard, with the traditional fare being home cooked, using fresh local produce.

ⓒ The Olive Branch

Main Street, Clipsham, Leics.
01780 410 355
www.theolivebranchpub.com

Satnav
LE15 7SH

Last orders for food: Weekdays: 2.00pm and 9.30pm. Sundays:3.00pm and 9.30pm.

£££

A deservedly award winning pub, but really a restaurant with comfortable dining areas. Mellow brickwork, sub-dued lighting and log fires give a cosy atmosphere. Excellent food with local pro-duce, including the famous Lincolnshire sausages. A well tended garden, so outside eating in the evening. The car park is adjacent, but take care driving out!

JUNCTIONS 34 TO 38

This part has a short section of motorway near Doncaster but otherwise it is dual carriageway throughout. From Grantham, it is flat open countryside. At Newark, you will cross over the River Trent, the historical divide between North and South England.

North of Doncaster, by the side of the road, is Robin Hood's Well, designed by Sir John Vanbrugh in 1710, which must have been his smallest building.

The condensing towers of the Ferrybridge Power Station have been a familiar landmark for generations.

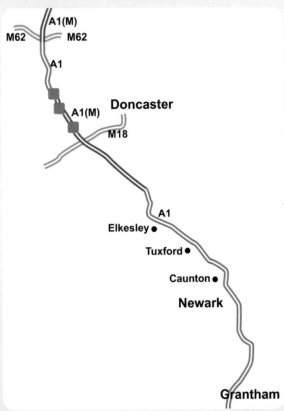

North of Newark there is a sign saying Caunton which is easy to use from both directions. Caunton is 3 miles to the west on a narrow road through some uninteresting countryside. The level crossing on the main line could add minutes to your journey! In the middle of the village

is a turning to the left by what was probably the blacksmiths. The Caunton Beck is on your left after a sharp bend.

 Caunton Beck

Main Street, Caunton, Notts.
01636 636 793
www.wigandmitre.com
Last orders for food: 8.00am to 9.30pm.

Satnav
NG23 6AB

££

A brick built range of buildings using old materials, it is now a comfortable restaurant with a bar. A cheerful atmosphere with a range of dining areas. Good wine list and traditional food with efficient and helpful service, especially after I had mislaid my mobile telephone.

The roundabout has been updated and rebuilt. Take the B1164 to Tuxford and the Mussel and Crab is 600 yards on the right.

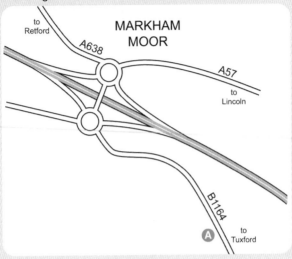

Mussel and Crab

Satnav
NG22 0PJ

Sibthorpe Hill, Tuxford, Notts.
01777 870 491
www.musselandcrab.com

Last orders for food: Weekdays: 2.30pm and 10.00pm. Sundays: 2.30pm and 9.00pm.

£££

A privately owned country restaurant in a converted farmhouse. One is treated to the sound of the sea on entering and goldfish look benignly down from a glass cistern in

the WC. There are several dining areas, in a modern style and traditional bar meals can also be had. Alfresco eating when the weather permits. Friendly efficient service and excellent fish dishes.

Coming from the south bear to the left marked Elkesley.
Through the village and the Robin Hood is on the right.
From the north it is more complicated as you will have to
get across the oncoming traffic and return the same way.

ELKESLEY

A6387

 ## The Robin Hood

Satnav
DN22 3AJ

High Street, Elkesley, Notts.
01777 838 259
www.robinhood.com

Last orders for food: 2.00pm and 9.00pm.
Sundays: 2.00pm. Mondays: Closed.

   £

A locals pub with a
Saloon Bar and a
dining area in the
former Lounge Bar.
Having said which it
is a friendly and
cheerful place and
the food is good and
reasonable.

JUNCTIONS 41 TO 56

This section has now been upgraded to motorway standards from Ferrybridge to Dishforth. The stretch from Dishforth to Leeming is now being upgraded and will be finished in 2012. It was going to be upgraded from there north to Scotch Corner, but this has been deferred for the time being.

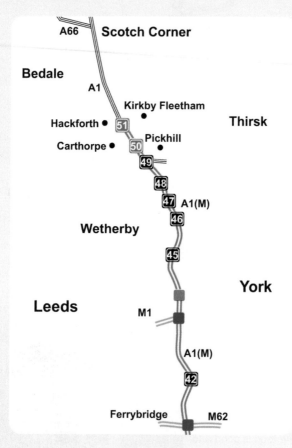

The approach to Ledsham has been altered since the upgrading of this section to a motorway. It is easier to find as there are feeder roads coming off the A1(M) in both directions.

Chequers Inn

Main Street, Ledsham, S. Yorks.
01977 683 135
www.chequersinn.co.uk

Satnav
LS25 5LP

Last orders for food: Weekdays and Saturdays: Noon to 9.15pm. Sundays: Closed.

££

A Free House in the middle of this Estate village. It is closed all day on Sunday because the lady of the manor in 1830 was abused on her way to church by estate workers pouring out of the pub. Bar meals downstairs and a comfortable restaurant above. The two chefs cook to order from an imaginative menu, the steak pie and lamb shanks are in demand.

Once off the motorway, head for Collingham. Just before you get there, Piccolino is on your left with a carpark.

Piccolino ★

Wetherby Road, Collingham, W.Yorks.
01937 579 797
www.piccolinorestaurants.co.uk

Satnav
LS22 5AY

Last orders for food:
Weekdays: Noon to 10.00pm. Sundays: Noon to 11.00pm (and Friday & Saturdays).

££

It has changed its name from La Locanda but otherwise it is exactly the same, as a popular Italian restaurant overlooking the river. There is a bar and some outside seating. The pasta and foccacia bread is baked on the premises. A cheerful atmosphere and children welcome.

For the Fox and Hounds turn right before Bickerton and then left at the T-junction in Walton. The pub is to the left on a sharp left hand bend.

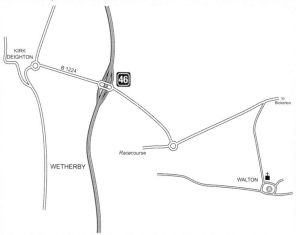

Ⓐ **The Fox and Hounds**
Hall Park Road, Walton, W. Yorks.
01937 842 192
www.thefoxandhoundswalton.com

Satnav
LS23 7DQ

Last orders for food:
Weekdays and Saturdays: 2.15pm and 9.15pm.
Sundays: 2.30pm. No evening meals.

                    £££

A thoroughly agreeable pub-cum-restaurant with friendly and efficient service. My crab soup with home-baked bread was good. Car park at rear, but take care coming out with a blind corner on the left, especially after such a good meal. It has changed hands, so comments please.

Take the A59 towards Knaresborough. After half a mile turn right to Coneythorpe. The Tiger is on your right as you come into the village.

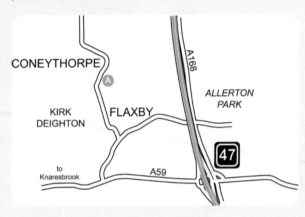

 The Tiger ★

Shortshill Lane, Coneythorpe, N.Yorks
01423 863 632
www.tiger-inn.co.uk

Satnav
HG5 0RY

Last orders for food: Noon to 9.00pm.
Sundays: Noon to 8.00pm.

££

A deservedly popular place as it is family owned and

Victoria will make sure that you are given a cheerful Yorkshire welcome. The dining room at the rear is decorated with stags heads, violins, fishing rods and walking sticks. My mussels, washed down with a glass of Pinio Grigio, were excellent and sensibly priced.

Boroughbridge is a market town and was a coaching stop on the Great North Road. To reach Stavely and Ferrensby take the A6055 to Knaresborough. For Roecliffe drive into the outskirts of Boroughbridge and take the road marked Roecliffe.

Places of interest

Newby Hall (17c &18c) HHA-8 miles.

Roman city of Isurium.

 **The Crown Inn** ★

High Street, Roecliffe, N.Yorks.
01423 322 300
www.crowninnroecliffe.com

Satnav
YO51 9LY

Last orders for food: 2.15pm and 9.00pm.
Sundays: Noon to 7.00pm.

£££

Originally a 16th century inn, it was bought recently by the previous owner of the Bay Horse at Kirk Deighton and he has made it into a friendly, comfortable and relaxed place to have a good meal. A restaurant to the left and a large bar area to the right of the front door. It was even more cheerful when I was there as there was a wedding party who seemed to be enjoying themselves.

B Royal Oak

Satnav
HG5 9LD

Main Street, Staveley, N. Yorks.
01423 340 267
www.royaloakstaveley.co.uk

Last orders for food:
Daily: 1.45pm and 8.45pm. Mondays: Closed.

 £

A Free House at the end of a rural village next to the church. A friendly atmosphere, even after I had walked out having forgotten to pay the bill! Eating areas as opposed to a restaurant.

C General Tarleton

Satnav
HG5 0PZ

Boroughbridge Road, Ferrensby, N. Yorks.
01423 340 284

Last orders for food: Weekdays: 2.15pm and 9.30pm. Sundays: Noon to 8.30pm.

 ££

A privately owned restaurant and hotel with contemporary furnished bedrooms. It is reputed to have the best cuisine in Yorkshire and gives a warm welcome from a young professional staff in a relaxed atmosphere. Children welcome.

The junction is not directly affected by the upgrading to motorway standard of the A1 to Leeming due to be finished in 2012. Turn off the road marked Asenby.

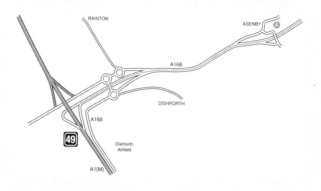

 **The Crab and Lobster** Satnav **YO7 3QL**
Main Street, Asenby, Thirsk, N. Yorks.
01845 577 286
www.crabandlobster.co.uk

Last orders for food: 2.00pm and 9.00pm.
Saturdays and Sundays: 2.00pm and 9.30pm.

£££

A quirky restaurant with a bar. One of the more unusual places for a stopover on a motorway! The décor has been done with imagination and the set menu (which obviously specialises in fish) is value for money. The Crab Manor Hotel next door is in the same ownership.

The Nags Head is now affected by the new motorway which will be completed in 2012. A Local Access Road 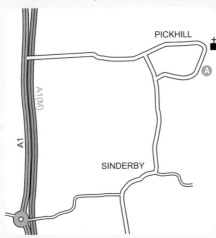 will run alongside the motorway from Baldersby to Leeming. Access to Pickhill is over the motorway from this road.

Nags Head

Main Street, Pickhill, N. Yorks.
01845 567 391
www.nagsheadpickhill.co.uk

Satnav
YO7 4JG

Last orders for food:
Weekdays: 2.00pm and 9.15pm.
Sundays: 2.00pm and 9.00pm.

£££

It really is a restaurant in an agricultural village with a separate dining room and bar meals at a well appointed bar. Good service and food. Breakfast available. You may need a deep pocket!

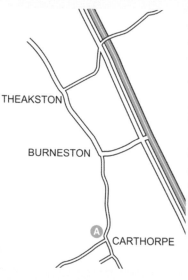

THEAKSTON

BURNESTON

 CARTHORPE

From the north, come off at the future Junction 51 at Leeming onto the A61, and then take the Local Access Road south. Come off where signed Burneston. Driving north, get off at Junction 50 at Baldersby on the Local Access Road.

Fox and Hounds

Main Street, Carthorpe, N. Yorks.
01845 567 433
www.foxandhoundscarthorpe.co.uk

Satnav
DL8 2LG

Last orders for food:
Daily: 2.00pm and 9.30pm. Mondays: Closed.

££

A village-pub-cum restaurant owned by Vince and Helen Taylor. They run a cheerful establishment serving high quality traditional fare in what was once the village smithy. The bellows and blacksmiths fire is still in evidence in the dining room.

The road to Hackforth is clearly signed from both directions off the dual carriageway. For the Black Horse, follow the turning to Kirkby Leetham further north.

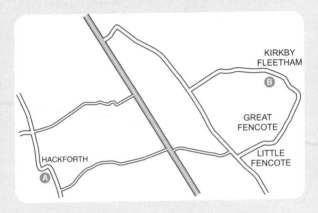

The Greyhound

Satnav
DL8 1PB

Main Street, Hackforth, N. Yorks.
01748 811 415

Last orders for food: Tuesday – Thursday: 3.00 and 9.00. Friday and Saturday: Noon to 9.00. Sunday: 4.00pm. Mondays: No meals.

£

A friendly village pub with a dining room and a bar. It has had a checkered ownership recently, but has settled back as a friendly village pub. They gave us a warm welcome when we arrived and we wish them good fortune in the future. A large chestnut tree outside gives shade to dogs in the car.

B Black Horse Inn

Satnav
DL7 0SH

Lumley Lane, Kirkby Fleetham, N. Yorks.

Last orders for food:
Tuesday to Thursday: 2.30pm and 8.30pm.
Friday and Saturday: 2.30pm and 9.30pm.
Sunday: Noon to 7.00pm.
Monday: No lunches. 8.30pm

£££

A village pub which has recently been well renovated with a restaurant and a stone flagged bar area. Classic dishes with hand pulled ales and good wines. A friendly staff who have worked hard to make it a success.

JUNCTIONS 56 TO 65

Not the most inspiring countryside but Durham Cathedral to the west is a World Heritage Site and is one of the most remarkable buildings in the country, known as "the loveliest building on Planet Earth".

The Angel of the North will greet you at the other end.

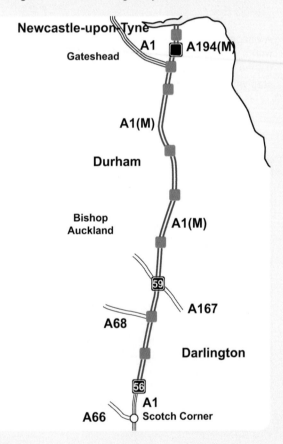

The building of the new motorway stretch has been deferred, so the old A1 dual carriageway will remain. Driving south from Scotch Corner take the first turn to the left marked Moulton. Going north, come off at Scotch Corner and turn right in Middleton Tyas.

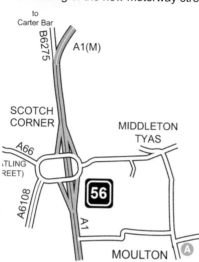

The Black Bull

Main Street, Moulton, N. Yorks.
01235 377 289
www.blackbullmoulton.com

Satnav
DL10 6QJ

Last orders for food: Monday to Friday: 2.30pm and 9.30pm. Saturdays: 2.00pm and 10.00pm. Sunday 4.00pm, no evening meals.

££/£££

For forty years it was the great traditional stopover for those travelling the Great North Road. The management has changed and there are plans to bring it into the 21st century. The old Pullman coach and private dining rooms will however remain but the bar will be more comfortable. It caters for the differing needs of visitors with a varied price range and menu.

Do not bear left on the roundabout but look out for the Aycliffe sign. At the traffic lights turn right. After some 30 yards turn right at the corner and The Country is 100 yards down on the left facing onto the green.

The County

Satnav
DL5 6LX

13 The Green, Aycliffe Village, Co. Durham
01325 312 273
www.thecountyaycliffevillage.com

Last orders for food:
Weekdays: 2.00pm and 9.15pm. Sundays: 3.00pm.

£££

A modernised country style pub on the village green. Tony Blair bought President Chirac of France to have dinner here. Restricted outside eating. French not essential. It has just changed hands.

Where the A1 diverges to the left, continue on the A194(M) to the first junction marked Washington. Keep left on the B1288. After 300 yards take the road to the right marked Springwell. Left at the first roundabout marked Wrekenton. Keep left until a T-junction and turn left. The brown sign for the hotel, which is past the riding school, is on the right.

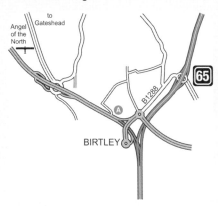

Bowes Incline Hotel ★

Satnav
DH3 1RF

Northside, Birtley, Co. Durham
01914 102 233
www.thebowesinclinehotel.co.uk

Last orders for food: Weekdays: Noon to 9.30pm. Sundays: Noon to 9.00pm.

   ££

It was bought by the present owners some four years ago and they have made it into a friendly, well managed hotel with a restaurant and bar meals within sight of the Angel of the North. The Bowes Incline was the name given to the now defunct colliery line to the docks on the Tyne.

A3(M) Horndean to Portsmouth

JUNCTIONS 1 TO 5

A short stretch of Motorway, which was completed in 1979 to ease the traffic flow at the junction of the A3 to the M27.

From Petersfield, the road climbs up to the high ground overlooking Portsmouth Harbour and the naval dock-yards. HMS Victory is dry docked there and the home of the Submarine Museum is over the harbour entrance at Gosport. Along the escarpment are a range of forts built by Palmerston in the 1860s to protect the coast against a possible invasion by the French.

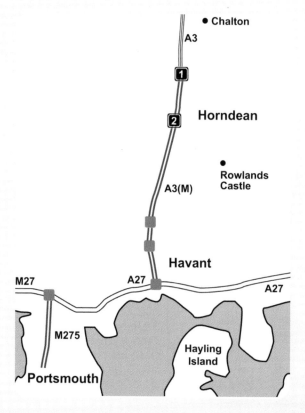

Driving south the turnoff for Chalton is 2 miles from the start of the motorway section. Going north it is more complicated as you will have to take a left turning signed Clanfield , follow along the dual carriageway for half a mile and then cross over. To continue your journey, go over the A3 and drive on north for about a mile.

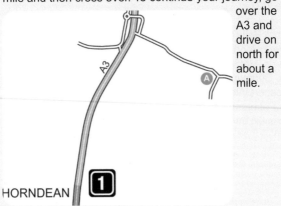

HORNDEAN **1**

Ⓐ **Red Lion** ★

South Lane, Chalton, Hants.
02392 592 246
www.fullers.com

Satnav
PO8 0BG

Last orders for food: Weekdays: Noon to 9.00pm. Sundays: Noon to 8.00pm.

££

Apparently it was first licensed in 1503 and is Hampshire's oldest pub. It has therefore low beams, panelled walls and inglenook fires. It is furnished with high backed traditional settles. There is a restaurant but bar meals are available. A friendly greeting and a good old fashioned atmosphere.

Get off at Junction 2. Carry on down the B2149 signed Westbourne. After the roundabout go through the woods and left to Rowlands Castle. There is another chance if you miss it further on.

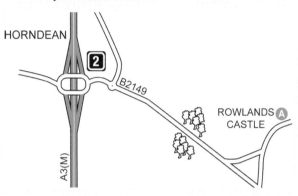

HORNDEAN

2

B2149

ROWLANDS
CASTLE

A3(M)

Places of interest

Stansted Park (1688-1903) HHA - 5m

 The Robin Hood Inn

Satnav
PO9 6AB

The Green, Rowlands Castle, Hants.
02392 412 268

Last orders for food: 2.30pm and 9.30pm.
Sundays: 3.15pm, no evening meals.

£££

A restaurant with a bar, it is just within five minutes form the junction. A friendly atmosphere light and airy, looking out over the village green. It has changed hands.

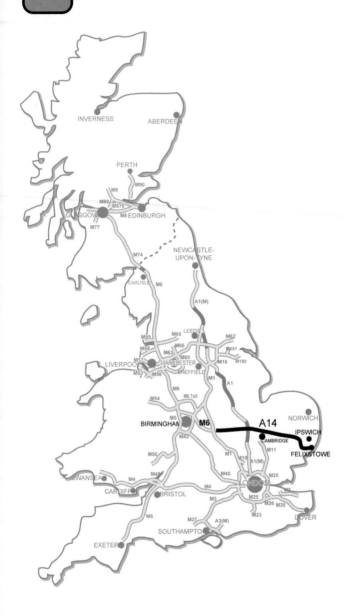

JUNCTIONS 1 TO 60

This is a dual carriageway rather than a motorway but all the junctions have now been numbered for easy recognition. It has become the main link between the Midlands and the port of Felixstowe.

M1 to Huntingdon

JUNCTIONS 1 TO 21

This section which connects the M1 to the A1 passes through the attractive rolling countryside of the Shires.

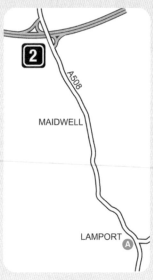

Take the A508 south through Maidwell and Lamport is about 2.5 miles further on.

Places of interest
Lamport Hall 17th-18th)
H.H.A. – 1m
Kelmarsh Hall (1732)
H.H.A. – 4m
Cottesbrooke Hall and Gardens (1702) H.H.A. – 6m

 The Swan

Harborough Road, Lamport, Northants.
01604 686 555
www.theswanlamport.co.uk

Satnav
NN6 9EZ

Last orders for food: 3.00pm and 9.00pm.
Sundays: No evening meals.

 ££

One of the new generation of restaurants with bar areas. Owned by McManus Taverns, it has been upgraded with modern décor and open spaces. It is efficient, with courteous service.

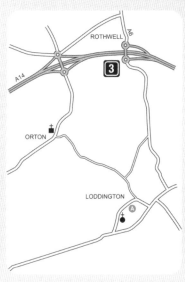

Head for the church
spire and the inn is
just to the north of it.

The Hare

Main Street, Loddington, Northants.
01536 710 337
www.thehareloddington.co.uk

Satnav
NN14 1LA

Last orders for food: Daily: 2.30pm and 9.30pm.
Sundays: 3.00pm, no evening meals.
Mondays: Closed.

££

A privately owned inn which
has a reputation for good
food and specialises in fish,
game and Aberdeen Angus
beef. For those in a hurry,
there are bar meals and
sandwiches. Outside seating
in a garden.

Come off at Junction 9 and take the country road south west to Pytchley – a name world famous amongst the hunting fraternity.

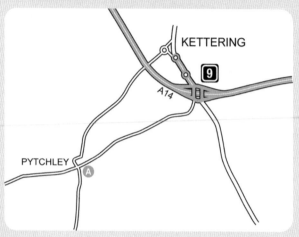

Ⓐ Overstones Arms ★

Satnav
NN14 1EU

Stringers Hill, Pytchley, Northants.
01536 790 215

Last orders for food: Daily: 2.00pm and 9.00pm.
Sundays: 2.30pm.

££

A traditional 18th century pub in the centre of a pictur-

esque village which was once a coaching inn. A large restaurant but bar meals are served. The speciality is the chestnut and stilton pate. Friendly welcome and good home cooked food.

No problems with the motorway signed junction. Go straight on at the first roundabout going north. After the second road to the right keep a lookout for the road into Lowick – which is sharper than that shown on the plan.

Places of interest
Lyveden New Bield (1595) NT – 7m

Ⓐ The Snooty Fox

Main Street, Lowick, Northants.
01832 733 434

Satnav
NN14 3BH

Last orders for food: Daily: 2.30pm and 9.00pm.
Mondays: Closed.

££

An upmarket pub-cum-restaurant in a range of old village houses, one being the old Manor House. They have been converted into a comfortable and well furnished hostelry. Original carved beams and a dining area near the bar, which is frequented by the natives. It is noted for its cooking. A garden in front for summer days.

For Keyston head south on the B663 towards Raunds. Zigzag through Keyston with the church on your right. At the end of the village turn right and The Pheasant is 100 yards on the left.

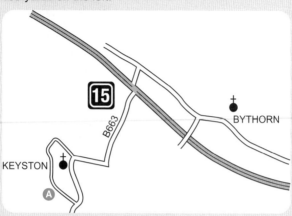

The Pheasant

Loop Road, Keyston, Cambs.
01832 710 241
www.thepheasant-keyston.co.uk

Satnav
PE28 0RE

Last orders for food: Daily: 2.30pm and 9.30pm.
Sundays: 2.30pm.

££

A restaurant with a bar area, which is now privately owned. Converted from a group of thatched cottages in this peaceful hamlet, it has been comfortably furnished with a lounge bar and three dining areas. A car park on the other side of the road. Outside seating in front as well as a garden.

Getting off and on when driving eastwards is easy, but more complicated driving westwards.

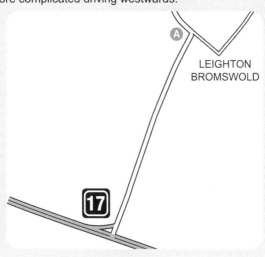

LEIGHTON
BROMSWOLD

 The Green Man

Satnav
PE28 5FJ

The Avenue, Leighton Bromswold, Cambs.
01480 890 238
www.greenmanpub.org

Last orders for food: Daily: 2.00pm and 9.00pm.
Sundays: 2.00pm. No evening meals.

££

A characterful pub-cum-restaurant, which was originally built in 1605, with low beams, log fires and old fashioned pub memorabilia. A friendly welcome from the family.

Drive to the village and the George Inn is on the left opposite the village green.

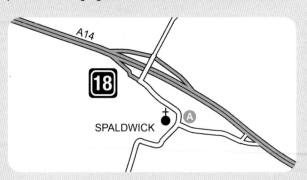

 SPALDWICK

The George Inn
High Street, Spaldwick, Cambs.
01480 890 293
www.thegeorgeofspaldwick.co.uk

Satnav
PE28 0TD

Last orders for food: 2.30 and 9.30pm.

££

This 16th century inn has been extensively refurbished.

However, there are still log fires and beams with a restaurant in the barn conversion. Well known for its black pudding. All produce is fresh and local.

No difficulty. Just head for the church.

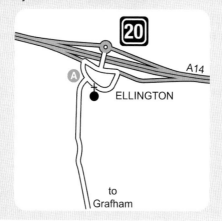

Places of interest
Grafham Water

 The Mermaid
High Street, Ellington, Cambs.
01480 891 450

Satnav
PE28 0AB

Last orders for food: Daily: 2.30pm and 9.00pm.
Sundays: No evening meals.

  ££

A traditional family
run old English pub
specialising in fish.
Built in the 13th cen-
tury, it has low
beams, log fires in
winter and serves
Real Ales. It has
changed hands.

JUNCTIONS 22 TO 42

Huntingdon is the Lord Protector, Oliver Cromwell's country with old villages in level countryside. Cambridge needs no introduction but should be visited even though car parking is a problem.

This part goes past Huntingdon, Cambridge and Newmarket to Bury St. Edmunds. It is a busy section, full of lorries and speed traps, especially where it joins the M11.

Newmarket is famous the world over for horse racing and the whole area is still given over to this purpose. There is a certain air of wealth and wellbeing. Going further east, the countryside changes to a more rural atmosphere with small villages and an air of timelessness.

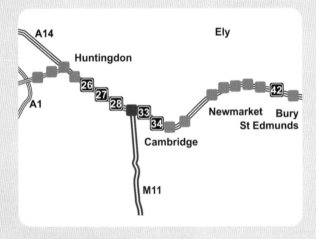

Junction 25 is the nearest to the village. For those going east it is the further of the staggered exits and vice versa. For the not so venturous come off at Junction 26 and take the first left.

The Cock ★

Satnav
PE28 9BJ

High Street, Hemingford Grey. Cambs.
01480 463 609
www.cambscuisine.com
Last orders for food: Weekdays: 2.30pm and 9.30pm. Sundays: 2.45pm and 8.30pm.

££

A traditional locals pub which has been stripped of more recent décor and given a new lease of life. The bar has a range of beer but an excellent meal or a light lunch can be had in the restaurant area with wooden floors and comfy chairs. The owners specialise in my favourite food - bangers and mash.

You can get to the King William IV by using either junction.

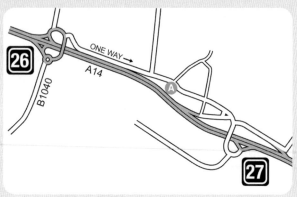

Places of interest

Capability Brown's home in Fenstanton.

King William IV

High Street, Fenstanton, Cambs.
01977 683 135

Satnav
PE28 9JF

Last orders for food: Daily: 3.00pm and 9.00pm.
Sundays: 3.00pm, no evening meals.
Summer (April to September): 8.00pm.

£

A cheerful 17th century pub in a picturesque village with a

friendly atmosphere with beams and inglenook fires. They specialise in home made puddings and sandwiches. It has changed hands and the new owners gave me a helpful welcome when I could not find Capability Brown's house in the village.

In Fenstanton, take a sharp right and then, after 600 yards, turn left, which is signed Fen Drayton.

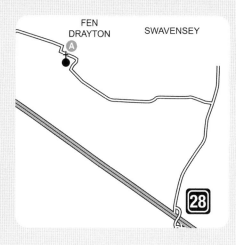

 **Three Tuns** ★
High Street, Fen Drayton, Cambs.
01954 750 018
www.the3tuns.co.uk

Satnav
CB24 4SJ

Last orders for food: Weekdays: 2.30pm and 9.30pm. Sundays: 2.30pm and 9.30pm.

£££

A charming family run pub, which was once the medieval Guildhall of the village. It still retains its traditional atmosphere with low beams and open fires. The menu is wide ranging and cooked to order if so required but baguettes and lighter fare can be had for those in a hurry. A large covered seating area outside for those brave enough to face the elements.

Junction 34 for Horningsea is for the benefit for those
driving east and then deciding to return westwards.
However help is at hand with Junction 33 as you can
use that to go in the required direction.

A Crown & Punchbowl ★ Satnav
CB25 9JG

High Street, Horningsea, Cambs.
01223 860 643
www.thecrownandpunchbowl.co.uk
Last orders for food: Weekdays: 2.30pm and
9.00pm. Sundays:2.30pm.

££

An old pub which has been given a modern makeover of

wooden floors, farmhouse tables and chairs and soft lighting. The low beams and
inglenook fire remain as does
the friendly service by the
helpful staff. There is no bar
as such but the food is excellent specialising in a variety of
sausages and fish. The bedrooms are clean and modern.

Head south from the junction signed Horringer. At the end of this village take a left and then first right at a cross roads. After a mile bear left at a Y junction to Whepstead.

Places of interest

Ickworth House (1795) NT- 3 miles.

White Horse ★

Rede Road, Whepstead. Suffolk
01284 735 760
www.whitehorsewhepstead.co.uk

Satnav
IP29 4SS

Last orders for food: Weekdays: 2.00pm and 9.30pm. Sundays: 2.00pm.

     £££

Garry and Di Kingshott have moved from the Beehive in Horringer and this old building has been renovated to make a traditional old inn with comfort and good service. The home made sausages are a speciality. Well behaved children are welcome and dog owners will be glad to hear that she has received an award from the local vet.

JUNCTIONS 43 TO 60

Bury St Edmunds was once the capital of East Anglia and the martyred King St Edmund is buried in St Edmundsbury Cathedral which still dominates the old town. He had been the patron saint of England until St George took over in more militant times. It is said that in 1214 various barons met at St Edmund's Altar and swore an oath that they would force King John to sign the Magna Carta.

The independent brewers Greene King, who run a string of good hostelries, have been brewing there since 1799.

East of Bury St Edmunds the countryside becomes increasingly more rural with thatched and plastered houses known as pargetting.

Ipswich is a fine traditional county town with a small port and some very interesting houses.

From there the A14 follows the line of the River Orwell to the busy international port of Felixstowe and the reason for so many lorries.

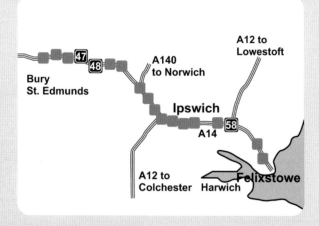

Take the A1088 to Norton and the Dog is on the right as you come into the village.

 The Norton Dog
Ixworth Road, Norton, Suffolk
01359 230 440

Satnav
IP31 3LP

Last orders for food: Daily: 2.00pm and 9.00pm.
Sundays: 2.00pm and 8.30pm.

£

A tenanted 16th century pub, which is part of the Greene King chain. Home cooked meals are served in the dining areas of bare brick walls and low beams.

You will have to cross over the central carriageway if coming from Felixstowe. Bear right at the entrance to the village. The Kings Arms is opposite.

Ⓐ Kings Arms

Satnav
IP14 3NT

Old Street, Haughley, Suffolk
01449 614 462

Last orders for food: Daily: 2.30pm and 8.30pm.

 £

A typical rustic old village inn with a plethora of beams.

There is a dining area with a log fire and the locals at the bar will tell you what is going on in the neighbourhood. The food is traditional with homemade pies, lasagne and fresh fish. A garden when warm.

The Ship is signposted from the main road. At Levington bear left and pass the church.

 The Ship

Church Lane, Levington, Suffolk
01473 659 573

Satnav
IP10 0LQ

Last orders for food: Daily: 2.00pm and 9.30pm.
Sundays: 3.00pm and 9.00pm.

££

An old inn with a smugglers room upstairs. Everything, including the biscuits, is homemade. They specialise in fish, which is served in the dining areas featuring nautical memorabilia. In the last hundred years, it has only changed hands four times. A garden where children and dogs must remain.

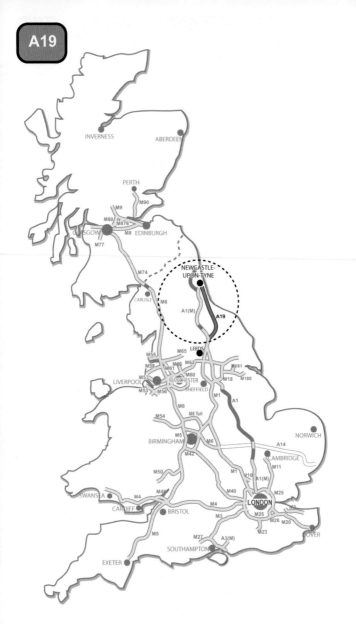

A19 Thirsk to Tyne Tunnel

The upgrading to motorway standard of the A1 between Dishforth and Leeming will mean traffic delays until the summer of 2012. I therefore decided to include the A19 in the guide which will hopefully bypass the problem. Although the exits are not numbered, it is a dual carriageway throughout and I always use it when travelling to or from Northumberland.

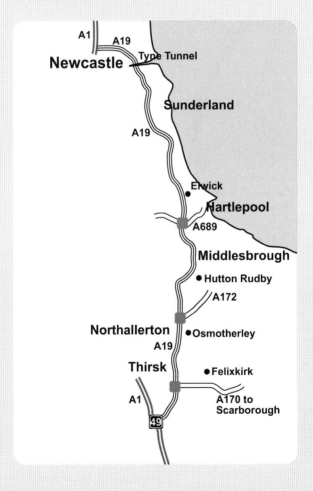

Come off the second junction to Thirsk and take the A170 to Scarborough. Just after you have crossed over the A19 bear left on the road signed Felixkirk and Boltby.

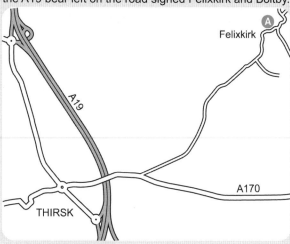

Places of interest
Thirsk is where the writer and vet James Herriott practised.

Carpenters Arms ★

Satnav
YO7 2DP

Felixkirk Road. Nr Thirsk, N.Yorks.
01845 537 369
www.carpentersarmsfelixkirk.com

Last orders for food: Weekdays: 2.00pm and 9.00pm. Sundays: 2.00pm. Mondays:Closed.

 ££

An 18c village pub at the foot of Sutton Bank where mother and daughter team Linda and Karen Bumby have been making motorists, including myself, welcome for the past ten years. They specialise in fish dishes. Dogs and children welcome provided they behave themselves.

The A684 from Northallerton joins the A19 here. Osmotherley is on a minor road continuation of it. The village is attractive and is the starting point for many of the walkers trekking over the North York Moors.

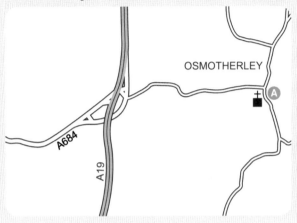

OSMOTHERLEY

The Three Tuns ★

Satnav
DL6 3BD

South End, Osmotherley, N.Yorks.
01609 883 301
www.threetunsrestaurant.co.uk

Last orders for food: Weekdays: 2.30pm and 9.30pm. Sundays: 3.00pm.

££

A family owned and run restaurant in this picturesque village in the North Yorkshire Moors. A well deserved reputation for high quality food in the Rennie Mackintosh inspired dining room. On warm days which we are told will be more often you can relax in the colourful garden. The bedrooms are comfortable for those wanting to spend longer in this part of the country.

Hutton Rudby is halfway between Middlesborough and Thirsk. It is signed off the A19 and is about 2 miles distant. It is an attractive village on the banks of the River Leven on the northern edge of the Cleveland Hills so easy access to the North Yorkshire Moors.

 The Bay Horse ★

Northside, Hutton Rudby, N.Yorks.
01642 700 252
www.thebayhorsehuttonrudby.co.uk

Satnav
TS15 0DA

Last orders for food: Weekdays: 2.00pm and 9.30pm. Sundays: 2.30pm.

££

A family owned and run locals pub which has changed hands. It is some 300 years old so is oak beamed with Yorkshire windows. An added attraction is the large garden for summer use or for getting ones breath back after a long walk.

An easy junction even though you may have to cross over the dual carriageway. Elwick is an attractive village with a large green like many villages in the north.

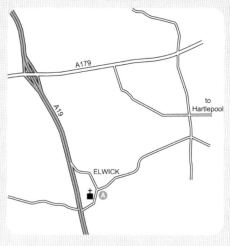

 Mcorville Inn ★

Satnav
TS27 3EF

34 The Green, Elwick, Cleveland
01429 273 344
www.themcorville.co.uk
Last orders for food: Daily:1.45pm and 9.00pm.
Sundays: 3.00pm.No evening meals.
Mondays: Closed.

 £

A locals' pub owned by Enterprise Inns in this attractive village. Dining areas dominated by a large bar but with a cheerful atmosphere. No dogs in the eating areas but children welcome.

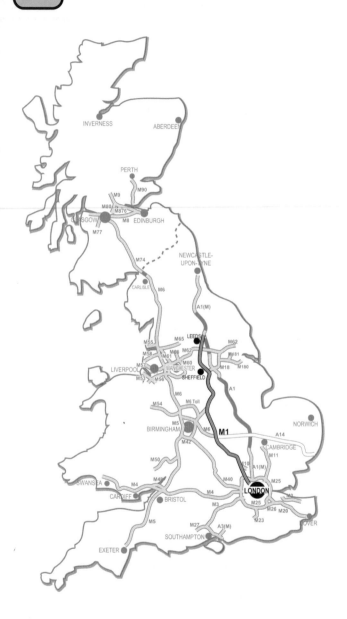

M1 London to Leeds

JUNCTIONS 8 TO 48

The M1 was the first major motorway to be built in the U.K. The first section of 72 miles was built by Messrs. Laing & Son at a cost of £50 million and was completed in 19 months. It was opened in November 1959 by the then Minister of Transport, Ernest Marples who, in real life, was a director of a building contracting firm. In 1965 a 70mph speed limit was imposed after it was being used as a test track by an Al Cobra Le Man car doing 183mph at 4am one wintry morning. The final link of the M1, from Leeds to the A1(M) of about 9 miles, was completed in 1999 at a cost of £140 million.

Hemel Hempstead to Crick

JUNCTIONS 8 TO 18

A congested section of the motorway until past the junction with the M6.

This is a sort of treasure hunt. The Angel in Toddington is easy. The Red Lion in Milton Bryan is still easy, but further. The French Horn in Steppingley does require determination. From the Red Lion to Church End, Ever-

sholt, over the motorway and there is The French Horn. You can return to Junction 12 from there on the scenic route.

The Angel

Luton Road, Toddington, Beds.
01525 872 380
www.angelpub.co.uk

Satnav
LU5 6DE

Last orders for food: Daily: Noon to 9.00pm.

£

Reputed to date from the 16th century it is a tenanted pub of the Greene King Brewery. Bar snacks are available, as is morning coffee. Well kept beer and immaculate WCs, according to a readers report.

ⓑ **Red Lion**

Satnav
MK17 9HS

Toddington Road, Milton Bryan, Beds.
01525 210 044
www.redlionmiltonbryan.co.uk

Last orders for food: Daily: 2.30pm and 9.30pm
Sundays: No evening meals.
Mondays: Closed in winter.

£££

A traditional restaurant-cum-pub. Home cooked food
with locally supplied meat and
fresh fish. The owner has
been in the business for many
years, and as a result it is a
friendly and efficient place,
hence the sign saying "Merry
meet and merry part, I drank
to thee with all my heart". The
recording studios where black
propaganda was beamed to
Germany are nearby.

ⓒ **The French Horn** ★

Satnav
MK45 5AU

Church End, Steppingley, Beds.
01525 720 122
www.thefrenchhornpub.com

Last orders for food: Weekdays: 2.00pm and
10.00pm. Sundays: Noon to 10.00pm.

£££

Originally a late 18th century
farmhouse it has been converted to give a warm welcome by the owners, into an
old world atmosphere of flagstoned floors, leather chairs
and wooden tables. There is
a spacious dining room but it
can get busy at peak periods,
so advisable to book.

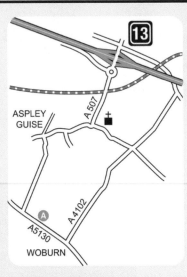

Turn left in the centre of Aspley Guise and then left again when you reach the A5130 towards Woburn.

The Birch

Newport Road, Woburn, Bucks.
01525 290 295
www.birchwoburn.com

Satnav
MK17 9HX

Last orders for food: Daily: 2.30pm and 10.00pm. Sundays: 5.00pm, no evening meals.

££

A privately owned wayside inn which is slightly reminiscent of Australian architecture. Its food is based on English and Continental menus and bar meals are available.

Nothing much to explain, as it is straightforward.

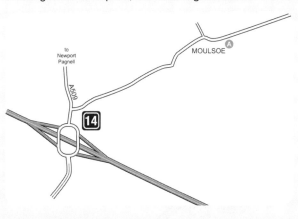

Places of interest
Bletchley Park – 6m

 Carrington Arms
Cranfield Road, Moulsoe, Bucks.
01908 218 050
www.thecarringtonarms.co.uk

Satnav
MK16 0HB

Last orders for food: Daily: 2.30pm and 10.00pm.
Saturdays and Sundays: Noon to 10.00pm.

£££

A smart restaurant with a bar,
which is part of a small group
of independent inns. Guests
choose from a selection of
prime cuts of Scottish steak,
fresh fish and seafood. It is
then cooked to their instruc-
tions on the charcoal grill and
served by young attentive
staff. Bar snacks also.

Junction 15 has been altered to give access to a large industrial estate and to have roundabouts on each side.

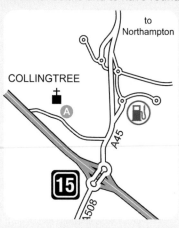

Follow the Northampton sign and Collingtree is on your left, so be alert. The nucleus of Collingtree is still an attractive village.

Places of interest
Stoke Park Pavilions (1630) Pte – 4 miles.

The Wooden Walls

High Street, Collingtree, Northants.
01604 764 082

Satnav
NN4 0NE

Last orders for food: Daily: 2.30pm and 9.00pm.
Sundays and Mondays: No evening meals.

£

A traditional old English pub with a dining area. A pleasant and cheerful atmosphere, serving Real Ales and bar meals to locals and passing motorists.

From the junction take the A45 to Flore. After less than a mile turn left to Nether Heyford.

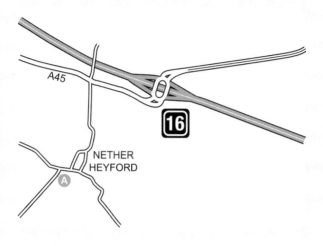

NETHER
HEYFORD

A Olde Sun ★

Satnav
NN7 3LL

Middle Street, Nether Heyford, Northants.
01327 340 164

Last orders for food: Daily: 2.00pm and 9.00pm.
Sundays: Noon to 8.00pm.

££

An old traditional 18th century pub which is not pretentious from the outside, but a warm welcome inside. An eclectic mix of brass bric a brac to keep visitors occupied. Bar meals from two bar areas available for lunch, but the restaurant is open in the evenings.

To get to Edwards, go straight on at the first roundabout and on again at the next one, over the canal and Edwards is on the banks of the canal to the right. For the others, take the A428 to the east and turn right at the first roundabout and left at the next. In Crick the Wheatsheaf is on the left and the Red Lion is on the right further on.

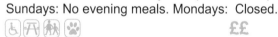

Ⓐ **Edwards**

West Haddon Road, Crick, Northants.
01788 822 517
www.edwardsrestaurant.co.uk

Satnav
NN6 7SQ

Last orders for food: Daily: 2.30pm and 9.30pm.
Sundays: No evening meals. Mondays: Closed.

££

A privately owned restaurant by the canal. Simple home cooking with fresh produce and served with the minimum of fuss. Dogs may appreciate a walk along the canal bank.

B The Red Lion

Satnav
NN6 7TX

Main Street, Crick, Northants.
01788 823 824

Last orders for food: Daily: 2.00pm and 9.00pm
Sundays: 2.00pm.

£

It has been a coaching inn since the early 1700s and is still family-run with a dining area. It is low beamed, as tall visitors will discover. Some outside seating and a car park at the rear. A congenial place where they pride themselves on their homemade steak pie with Real Ales.

C The Wheatsheaf ★

Satnav
NN6 7TU

Main Road, Crick, Northants.
01788 823 824

Last orders for food: Daily: 2.30pm and 9.00pm.
Sundays: 4.00pm. No evening meals.

£

A village pub near the church. It is a tenanted pub of Scottish and Newcastle, with a restaurant to the rear of the garden. You can have a friendly chat with the locals in the bar.

JUNCTIONS 19 TO 29

This seems to be a culinary desert, but there are some places worthy of a stopover.

There are however, some interesting places to see off the motorway, such as Stanford Hall and the Civil War battlefield of Naseby off Junction 19.

At Junction 27 is Lord Byron's old home of Newstead Abbey, which he sold in 1816 when he went abroad. Lastly, there are those stupendous buildings of Hardwick Hall, Bolsover Castle, Sutton Scarsdale and further afield, Haddon Hall and Chatsworth.

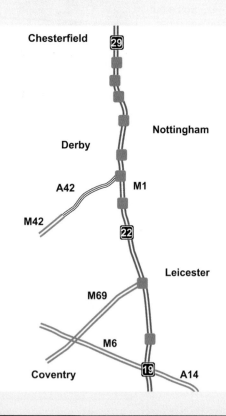

For those driving south follow the signs marked A19 Felixstowe. Turn left at the first roundabout for Swinford. For those driving north - it is complicated. You can either go to Junction 20 and head back – or else take the M6 to Junction 1 and do the same or else drive on.

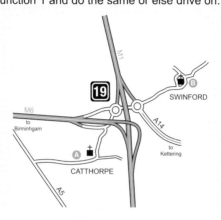

Ⓐ The Chequers

High Street, Swinford, Leics.
01788 860 318
www.chequersswinford.co.uk

Satnav
LE17 6BL

Last orders for food: Daily: 2.00pm and 9.00pm.
Sundays: No evening meals.
Mondays: Closed for lunch.

£

A traditional friendly village pub with pub games and gas log fires. Meals are served in the bar with Real Ales or in the dining area. Garden and a playground.

Could not be easier to find. Take the dual carriageway towards Markfield for 1.5 miles and at the first roundabout the Field Head Hotel is facing you.

Field Head Hotel

Markfield Lane, Markfield, Leics.
01530 245 454
www.thefieldhead.com

Satnav
LE67 9PS

Last orders for food: Weekdays: Noon to 10.00pm. Sundays: Noon to 9.00pm.

££

A modern hotel but with all the plusses of being near the motorway. Friendly and efficient service. A spacious bar for a quick meal and several restaurant areas. Outside seating in the courtyard.

The junction is studded with brown signs of the Tourist Board to all the great houses in the vicinity. The sign to Heath for the Elm Tree off the A6175 to the right is not easy to see. For the other two, take the small road opposite to the left and continue along until you go under the motorway. Hardstoft is to the right and bear left for the Hardwick Inn and Hardwick Hall.

Places of interest

Hardwick Hall (c 1597) NT – 2 miles
Bolsover Castle (c1620) EH – 1 mile
Chatsworth (c1552-1820) – 15 miles
Sutton Scarsdale (c1720) – 1 mile
Haddon Hall (c1380 to 17th C) – 17 miles

 Elm Tree
Mansfield Road, Heath, Derbys.
01246 850 490
www.theelmtreeheath.co.uk

Satnav
S44 5SE

Last orders for food: Weekdays: 2.00pm and 9.00pm. Saturdays and Sundays: Noon to 8.00pm.

££

A restaurant with a bar. It was in the first edition, but I took it out as it was getting tired. After a friend of mine had lunched there recently, I called in with some trepidation on my return north. I found that there had been a makeover and it was now a comfortable place with much more room and space. The soup was particularly good and the service was friendly.

The Hardwick Inn

Satnav
S44 5QJ

Hardwick Park, Derbys.
01246 850 245
www.hardwickinn.co.uk

Last orders for food: Daily: Noon to 9.30pm.
Sundays: Noon to 9.00pm.
Mondays: Bar meals only.

£££

Built in the 17th century
it has been converted
into a popular place to
eat with several dining
areas. Plenty of outside
seating. It could become
crowded during the sum-
mer. Dogs outside.

 ## Famous Shoulder ★

Satnav
S45 8AF

Chesterfield Road, Hardstoft, Derbys.
01246 850 276

Last orders for food: Daily: 2.30pm and 9.30pm.
Sundays: 3.00pm.

£££

It was previously known as the
Weeping Ash and was listed
in the early editions. My
stepson spent a night there
and was underwhelmed, but
when I went back, new owners had taken it on and it was
much improved. However,
they are going to lease it to
an individual shortly, so comments would be appreciated.

JUNCTIONS 30 TO 48

Here again there seems to be few, if any, worthwhile places to stop and rest. This is a pity as at this stage of the journey you will be looking for just such a stop.

There are places however to see on the way. These include the Cannon Hall Museum off Junction 37. Near Junction 46 there is Harewood House and also Temple Newsam House which is known as the Hampton Court of the North.

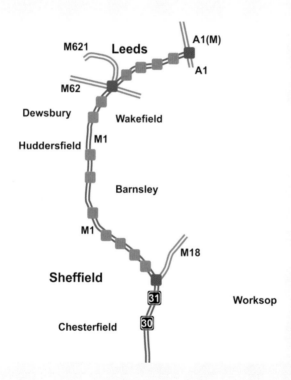

Head for Barlborough and then the church.

BARLBOROUGH

Places of interest
Renishaw Hall Gardens (1625) HHA – 3 miles
Barlborough Hall (18th C) Pte – 1 mile

The Rose and Crown

Satnav **S43 4ET**

High Street, Barlborough, Derbys.
01246 810 364

Last orders for food: Daily: 2.00pm and 9.00pm.
Sundays: No evening meals.

 ££

A cheerful village pub cum restaurant owned by Greene King. It was in the original edition, but subsequently did not make the grade and was dropped. It has now had a change of ownership, so comments please.

After 100 yards turn right by the Fire Station, The Yellow
Lion is on the right.

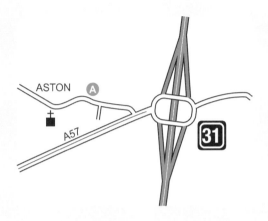

ASTON Ⓐ

A57

31

Ⓐ **The Yellow Lion**

Satnav **S26 2EB**

Worksop Road, Aston cum Aughton, S. Yorks.
01142 872 283

Last orders for food: Daily: Noon to 9.00pm.

£

A simple locals pub
with stone flagged
floors in a built up
area, but overlook-
ing fields. It serves
home cooked bar
meals. One Armed
Bandits and a Pool
Table for wet days.

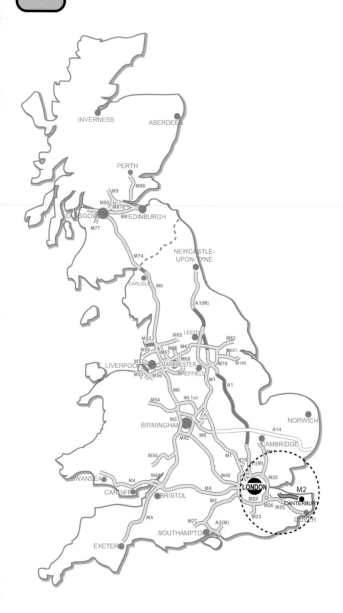

JUNCTIONS **2** TO **7**

One of the shorter motorways, being only 25 miles in length, but was one of the first to be built in 1963.

It was designed to create a faster journey between London and the Channel Ports, linking up with existing roads. The approach to London however remained abysmal. The connecting road from the Blackwall Tunnel and Greenwich and the link with the M25 has been much approved.

The traffic density was reduced after the construction of the M20 to the south but you can interchange easily between the two should the conditions become unbearable.

The motorway passes some historic towns such as Rochester, the setting for the Pickwick Papers by Charles Dickens; the old Naval Dockyards at Chatham burnt by the Dutch in 1667 and the ancient city of Canterbury, settled by the Romans and where Saint Augustine introduced Christianity to the country in AD 597 and where Thomas a Becket was murdered in 1173.

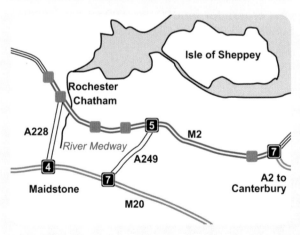

Easy enough to get to Stockbury, as there is a gap in the dual-carriageway opposite the turning off.

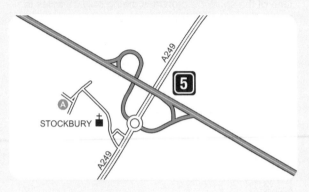

Places of interest

Stockbury features in the Doomsday Book in 1086 as Stochinberge.

 ## The Harrow Inn

The Street, Stockbury, Kent
01795 842 546

Satnav
ME9 7UH

Last orders for food: Daily: 2.00pm and 9.00pm.
Sundays: 3.00pm and 8.00pm. Mondays: Closed.

             ££

A typical 200 year old country pub opposite the village green. A small dining area and a snack menu at the bar. Seating in the garden. In the past Morris Dancing has taken place on the green in summer and it is hoped that it will continue.

Continue on the A299 towards Whitstable. After some
two miles turn off on a minor road signed Fostall and
Hernhill. Right at the T junction and then left after 400
yards to Hernhill. The Red Lion is on the crossroads in
the centre of the village.

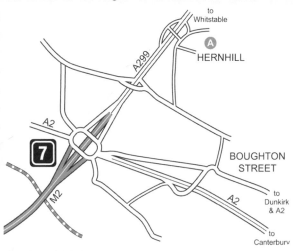

 Red Lion

The Green, Hernhill, Kent.
01227 751 207

Satnav
ME13 9JR

Last orders for food: Daily: 2.00pm and 9.00pm.
Sundays: Noon to 7.30pm.

£££

A privately owned half-
 timbered 14th Century pub.
Traditional meals are served
in the bar areas with a log
fire, but there is also a
restaurant upstairs for
evening meals. A garden for
summer seating and a sun-
dial dating from 1364 to
speed you on your way. It
has changed hands.

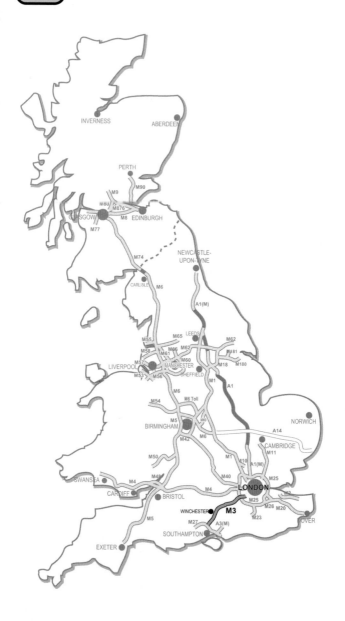

JUNCTIONS 1 TO 12

This motorway connects London with the port at Southampton; the A31 to Bournemouth and with the south west of England by way of the A303.

The building of the continuation of the motorway past Winchester in 1994 meant the cutting of a trench at Twyford Down. This caused massive unrest by protestors and increased subsequent cost. It might have been cheaper to build a tunnel. The motorway passes Basingstoke, a new town which has managed to destroy any vestige of what had once been a pleasant market town. Winchester however retains its historic atmosphere and is therefore full of visitors.

A simple junction and the pub is easy to find.

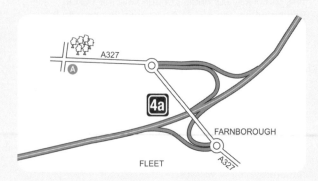

Places of interest
Napoleon III's Mausoleum, Farnborough – 3 miles
Airborne Forces Museum, Aldershot - 4 miles

 Crown and Cushion
Minley Road, Yateley, Hants.
01252 545 253

Satnav
GU17 9UA

Last orders for food: Weekdays: 3.00pm and
9.00pm. Saturdays and Sundays: Noon to 9.00pm.

     ££

An attractive rural
pub in a wooded
area on the way to
Yateley Common.
It serves traditional
meals in the bar, or
else in the beer gar-
den, which has
heaters should the
weather be in-
clement.

From the junction take the A287 to the A30. Continue over and then left to Newnham. Turn right in the centre signed Rotherwick. Down the main street there and it will be on the right.

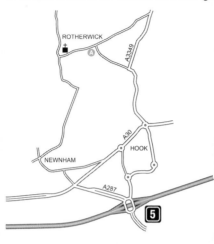

 The Falcon Inn ★

Satnav
RG27 9BL

The Street, Rotherwick, Hants.
01256 762 586
www.thefalconrotherwick.co.uk

Last orders for food: Weekdays: 2.30pm and 9.30pm. Sundays: 3.00pm.

££

A 300 year old pub set in tranquil country-side which has been modernised and now has a restaurant. It caters for locals, passing motorists or any other good sorts.

M3 **7** Basingstoke A30
Newbury (A339)

Not a difficult junction

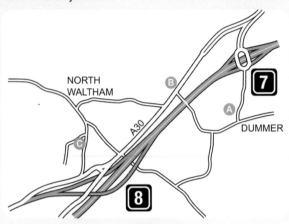

NORTH WALTHAM

A30

DUMMER

Ⓑ Ⓐ **7**

Ⓒ

8

Places of interest
The Grange (18th C) EH - 8 miles

Ⓐ **Queen Inn**

Down Street, Dummer, Hants.
01256 397 367
www.thequeendummer.com

Satnav
RG25 2AD

Last orders for food: Daily: 2.30pm and 9.30pm.
Sundays: 9.00pm.

                                          ££

A popular and well
known family owned
pub. It gets its name
from the fourth wife of
Henry VIII who was
Anne of Cleaves, the
Mare of Flanders.
There is a garden at
the back where dogs
are welcome.

ⓑ **The Sun Inn** ★

Satnav
RG25 2DJ

Winchester Road, North Waltham, Hants.
01256 397 234
www.suninndummer.com

Last orders for food: 2.00pm and 9.00pm.
Fridays, Saturdays and Sundays: 2.30pm.
No evening meals on Sundays.

£

Once a coaching inn on the
old A30, it has had a
makeover after being bought
by Mike and Laura Doyle and
is a cheerful, busy place
where children and dogs are
welcome.

ⓒ **The Fox Inn** ★

Satnav
RG25 2BE

Popham Lane, North Waltham, Hants.
01256 397 288
www.thefox.org

Last orders for food: Weekdays: 2.30pm and 9.30.
Sundays: 3.00pm.

££

An old vernacular Hampshire
flint-stone house overlooking
quiet farming country- side.
It is privately owned and has
built up a reputation for
home-sourced food and has
made special provision for
children. A heated patio for
inclement weather and log
fires when in extremis.

From the junction take the A34 towards Sutton Scotney.
After 1 mile take the slip road on the A30 towards Basingstoke. At the end of the dual carriageway bear right
on the A3047 towards New Alresford. After two miles,
before Martyr Worthy, turn right to Easton.

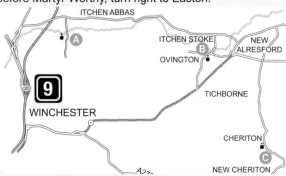

Places of interest
The Grange (18th C) EH - 8 miles

ⒶChestnut Horse

Main Road, Easton, Hants.
01962 779 257
www.thechestnuthorse.com

Satnav
SO21 1EG

Last orders for food: Daily: 2.00pm and 9.30pm.
Sundays: 4.00pm. No evening meals.

  ££

A tenanted pub of Hall &
Woodhouse, so a good
range of beers. An old 16th
Century building with low
beams, log fires and a cheerful atmosphere. Traditional
cooking and friendly service.
Outside seating on a terrace
at the rear for summer days.

Bush Inn ★

Satnav
SO24 0RE

East Lane, Ovington, Hants.
01962 732 764
www.thebushinn.co.uk

Last orders for food: 2.00pm and 9.00pm.
Fridays, Saturdays and Sundays: 2.30pm.
No evening meals on Sundays.

   ££

A four roomed country pub at the end of a quiet lane on
the banks of the River Itchen
with a large garden for summer days. Bar meals in the
dining areas and an interesting collection of photographs
and rural memorabilia. A
cheerful and cosy atmosphere
with friendly service. It won
the Hampshire Pub of the
Year Award recently.

The Flower Pots ★

Satnav
SO24 0QQ

The Goodens, Cheriton, Hants.
01962 771 318
www.flowerpots.f2s.com

Last orders for food: Weekdays: 2.30pm and 9.30.
Sundays: 3.00pm.

   ££

Once a Georgian private
house it now provides good
wholesome food in the various rooms. Until recently
beer was brewed on the
premises but the range of
beers on offer are as good as
ever as is the warm welcome.

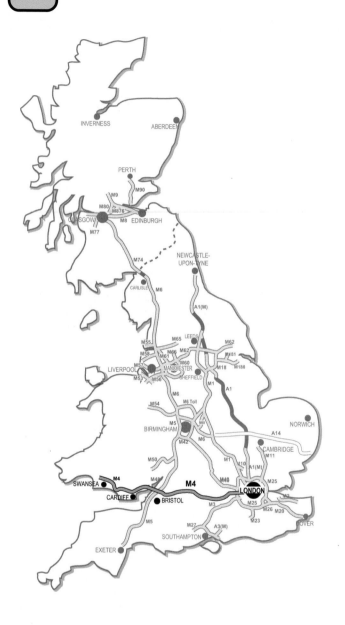

JUNCTIONS 8/9 TO 49

The M4, which is 121 miles long, is the fourth longest motorway in the UK. It is a direct link from London to South Wales and interconnects with the M5 north of Bristol. The first section, the Chiswick Flyover, was opened in 1959 by a blonde starlet called Jayne Mansfield. The last part was completed in 1973. It may be continued to Fishguard at some future date, instead of terminating in a rather bleak part of South Wales. It passes through some of the most varied scenery in southern England.

Windsor to Hungerford

JUNCTIONS 8/9 TO 14

This section of the motorway follows along the Thames Valley past Reading and Newbury before rising up to the open expanses of the Marlborough Downs.

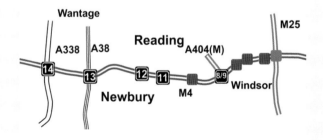

Take the spur road A308(M) to the roundabout. Turn right towards Windsor and take the left turn to Bray before going under the motorway. For Holyport take the A330 signed Winkfield Row. Turn left at the village green and The Belgian Arms is 200 yards on the left.

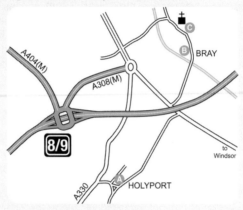

Ⓐ The Belgian Arms

Holyport Street, Holyport, Berks.
01628 634 468
www.thamesideevents.com

Satnav
SL6 2JR

Last orders for food: Daily: 2.30pm and 9.30pm.
Sundays: 3.00pm. No evening meals.

££

A popular pub on the edge of the village green by a duck pond. There is a large garden where you can sit and dogs and play. Fish specials daily. You will have to ask why it is called The Belgian Arms.

B The Crown Inn ★

Satnav
SL6 2AH

High Street, Bray, Berks.
01628 621 936

Last orders for food: Weekdays: 2.00pm and 9.00pm. Sundays: 3.30pm and 8.30pm

££

A small low beamed pub with a large and secluded garden at the rear for outside seating in the summer. The staff are friendly and helpful and it has a cheerful atmosphere. It has just been sold.

C The Hinds Head ★

Satnav
SL6 2AB

High Street, Bray, Berks.
01628 626 151
www.thehindsheadhotel.com

Last orders for food: Weekdays: 2.30pm and 9.30pm. Sundays: 400pm

£££

A low-ceilinged, wooden pan-elled Tudor building which is in the centre of this pictur-esque village. It is owned by the TV celebrity chef Heston Blumenthal who also has the Fat Duck further down the street. The prices luckily for the passing motorist is not comparable although the standard is still high.

At the roundabout turn left to Three Mile Cross, but avoid getting onto the dual carriageway. This junction has been recently upgraded and is therefore more complicated.

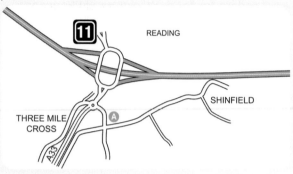

Places of interest
Silchester (Calleva Atrebartum) - 7 miles

 The Swan

Basingstoke Road, Three Mile Cross, Berks.
01189 883 674
www.theswan-3mx.co.uk

Satnav **RG7 1AT**

Last orders for food: Daily: 2.15pm and 9.30pm. Sundays: 2.00pm.

££

Traditional Free House with a dining area, as well as

serving bar meals and washed down with Real Ales. There is some outside seating and a beer garden beyond the large car park. The resident Irish Wolfhound, Mr Doyle, is the mascot of the London Irish Rugby Football Club. A recent addition is a large patio with its own bar.

At the roundabout turn right to Theale, which is a surprisingly attractive little town. It is so named as it was the second night's stop out of London for wagoners and was called The Ale. It certainly seems to have more than its fair share of pubs and hotels, so if the one mentioned below is full, there are alternatives.

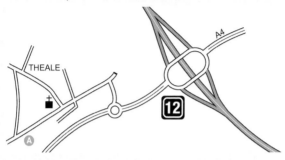

Places of interest

Engelfield House Garden HHA - 3 miles
Basildon Park (1776-1783) NT - 7 miles

Ⓐ The Volunteer

Church Street, Theale, Berks.
01189 302 489

Satnav
RG7 5BX

Last orders for food: Daily: Noon to 9.00pm.
Sundays: 4.00pm, no evening meals.

£

Traditional old pub serving bar meals with home cooking. An interesting collection of military and sporting prints.

The Junction has become a major interchange. For Chievely bear first left off the A34 to Oxford. The Olde Red Lion is on the left as you come into the village. For Winterbourne continue on. Left on the B4494 and first right after the motorway. From there to The Red House continue on the minor road – drive under the dual carriageway A34 – right on the A4 and take the road signed Marsh Benham to the left. The Red House is on the left. It is quicker to take the A34 and A4.

Ye Olde Red Lion ★

Satnav
RG20 8XB

Cold Ash Hill, Chievely, Berks.
01635 248 379
www.yeolderedlion.com

Last orders for food: Weekdays: 2.30pm and 9.30pm. Sundays: 3.00pm and 9.00pm.

££

An old locals pub with a restaurant which has an imaginative menu. The bar has a collection of curios and warmed by a fire. Outside there is seating on warmer days. It has featured in earlier editions, but reappears as it is good value for money.

Winterbourne Arms ★ Satnav RG2 8BB

Main Road, Winterbourne, Berks.
08712 239 362

Last orders for food: Weekdays: 3.00pm and
10.00pm. Sundays: 4.00pm

££

Used to be known as
the New Inn probably
because its history goes
back 300 years when it
was a bakery. This
country hostelry in a
rural village has a good
restaurant but there is a
bar for simpler meals.

The Red House

Satnav
RG20 8LY

Main Road, Marsh Benham, Berks.
01635 582 017
www.redhousepub.com
Last orders for food: Daily: 3.00pm and 9.30pm.
Sundays: 4.00pm and 9.30pm.

£££

A privately owned elegant
restaurant in a thatched
house, with an adjoining bar.
Outside seating in the garden. English and Continental
cuisine using local produce
either a la carte in the
restaurant or with a Bistro
menu. Traditional French
cooking with a modern twist.

An easy junction. Follow the sign to Lambourn for the
Pheasant Inn.

Places of interest
Ashdown House (c1690) NT - 9 miles

Ⓐ **The Pheasant Inn**

Satnav **RG17 7AA**

Ermine Street, Shefford Woodlands, Berks.
01488 648 284
www.thepheasantinnlambourn.co.uk

Last orders for food: Daily: 2.30pm and 9.30pm

££

It has always been a popular rendezvous and has re-

cently been renovated and
now has eleven bedrooms. It
includes a restaurant with an
excellent chef, so food is
taken seriously. The fish
comes daily from Cornwall.
Bar snacks are available. It is
a pleasant place, especially
for the racing fraternity.

JUNCTIONS 15 TO 22

From Junction 15 to Junction 18, the motorway goes through the southern part of the Cotswolds. From Junction 18 it descends towards the River Severn.

Swindon was the centre of the locomotive workshops for the Great Western Railway and is now a modern commercial town with a railway museum. Chippenham, once a picturesque market town, has now been modernised out of all recognition. Bath, off Junction 18, is famous for its Georgian architecture.

In 1996 the second Severn Bridge was completed to cope with the increased traffic. The old bridge crossing was then renamed the M48 and the new section became the M4. The M49 link to Avonmouth is best avoided if seeking a meal

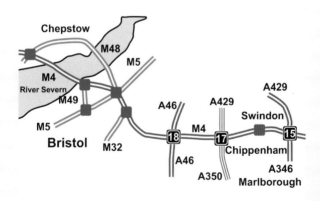

to Swindon

CHISELDON

5 miles

OGBOURNE ST GEORGE

OGBOURNE ST ANDREW

to Marlborough

The Plough Inn is 200 yards from the junction on the A346 to Marlborough. The Patriots Arms is in Chiseldon but easy to find. The Silks on the Downs is 5 miles from the junction on the Marlborough road and is on the right hand side.

Ⓐ **Plough Inn** ★

Marlborough Road, Badbury, Wilts.
01793 740 342

Satnav
SN4 0EP

Last orders for food: Weekdays: 2.00pm and 9.15pm. Sundays: 3.00pm.

£

A tenanted pub of Arkells which has been renovated and is well run by Mark Beales. Being so close to the motorway junction it is ideal for those who just want a quick meal before dashing on. A patio for those wanting fresh air.

ⓑ **Chiseldon House Hotel**

Satnav
SN4 0NE

New Road, Chiseldon. Wilts.
01793 741 010
www.chiseldonhousehotel.co.uk

Last orders for food: Daily: 2.00pm and 9.15pm.
Sundays: 2.00pm. Light evening meals.

£££

An 18th century former
manor house which
has been converted
into a privately owned
hotel with extensive
gardens. A restaurant
in the Orangery and a
bar for quicker meals.

ⓒ **Silks on the Downs** ★

Satnav
SN8 1RZ

Main Road, Ogbourne St Andrews, Wilts.
01914 102 233

Last orders for food: Weekdays: 2.30pm and
9.30pm. Sundays: 2.30pm.

£££

Those in the racing fraternity will know why it is called
Silks. For the others you will
have to go there and see. It is
a comfortable and roomy
restaurant with a garden at
the rear. It has modern
wooden tables and chairs
and a very friendly service.
My crab cakes were espe-
cially good. The menu gives
an amusing run down on all
the staff.

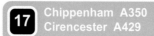

The Hit or Miss in Kington Langley could be missed, which would be a pity. Take the narrow road when you come off the roundabout. Norton is harder to find but follow the signs and the same could be said for Grittleton.

Places of interest

Bowood House (c1720-1760) HHA - 6 miles
Lack Abbey (1232-1540) NT - 7 miles
Corsham Court (1582) HHA - 9 miles

 The Hit or Miss

Satnav
SN15 5NS

Days Lane, Kington Langley, Wilts.
01249 758 830

Last orders for food: Weekdays: 2.30pm and 9.30pm. Sundays: 2.30pm and 8.30pm.

££

A popular village pub with a restaurant, dating from the

18th Century in the centre of this scattered hamlet. There is a friendly welcome to all, including dogs and it has an imaginative menu with local game. A good ambiance. Some outside seating for summer use.

Ⓑ The Vine Tree ★

New Road, Chiseldon. Wilts.
01666 837 654
www.thevinetree.co.uk

Satnav
SN16 0JP

Last orders for food: Weekdays: 2.30pm and
9.30pm. Sundays: 2.30pm.

£££

A Free House with character. A
cosy atmosphere with beams,
flagged floors and carpets. The
staff are friendly and efficient and
it specialises in fish. The crab,
which I can personally recom-
mend, is brought in daily from
Kyzance Cove in Cornwall.

Ⓒ Neeld Arms

The Street, Grittleton, Wilts.
01249 782 470
www.neeldarms.co.uk

Satnav
SN14 6AP

Last orders for food: Daily: 2.00pm and 9.30pm.

££

A Free House owned by Charlie & Boo West. It is still a locals village pub, but now has
a restaurant with traditional
meals. A cheerful and friendly
place and ideal for those coming to Mary Howard's Gift Fair
at Hullavington.

The Bull seems further than it is. The Tollgate is down the road from The Crown if tea beckons.

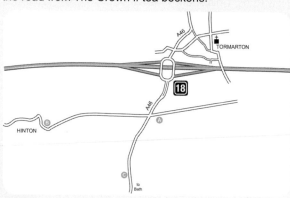

Places of interest
Dyrham Park (1691) NT - 1 mile
Horton Court (c1690) NT - 7 miles

Ⓐ **The Crown**
Dyrham, Glos.
01225 891166
ohhcompany.co.uk

Satnav
SN14 8HZ

Last orders for food: Daily: 2.15pm and 9.30pm.

            ££

A country pub come restaurant just two minutes from Junction 18. Once a coaching stop in the 1700's, it still gives a friendly welcome and serves home cooked meals. A childrens playground and garden where dogs are allowed.

Ⓑ Bull Inn

Satnav
SN14 8HG

Hinton, Glos.
01179 372 332
Last orders for food: Daily: 2.00pm and 9.00pm.
Sundays: 3.00pm and 8.30pm
Mondays: No lunches.

££

A friendly village pub with two
large fireplaces for winter
nights, a restaurant and a
large garden. All food is
cooked on the premises.
It is highly rated by other
motorists.

Ⓒ Tollgate Teashop ★

Satnav
SN14 8LF

Oldfields Gatehouse, Dyrham, Glos.
01225 891 585
www.tollgateteashop.com
Last orders for food: Daily: 9.30am to 5.00pm.
Summer weekends: 9.30am to 6.00pm.
Mondays: Closed.

£

A small and cosy privately-
owned teashop which was
once a Toll House. Light
lunches and old-fashioned
teas with clotted cream. Outside seating at the rear, with
views to the Welsh hills,
where dogs are welcome. A
good breakfast is available.

JUNCTIONS 23 TO 49

As the map suggests there are few places where it is worth leaving the motorway to eat, which may account for the large number of service stations. There are how-ever, plenty of places of interest to see.

Caerleon off Junction 24 is the site of Isca, the Roman base of the II (Augusta) Legion from Spain. In Cardiff, the regional capital of Wales, the Castle is built on the walls of the Roman fort, whilst to the north there is Castell Coch, both restored by the 3rd Marquess of Bute in the 19th Century with the help of the architect, William Burges. Some six miles beyond Castell Coch to the east are the imposing ruins of Caerphilly Castle, mute evidence of the occupation by Edward I. Nearby is Caer-went, the old Roman capital of Silures.

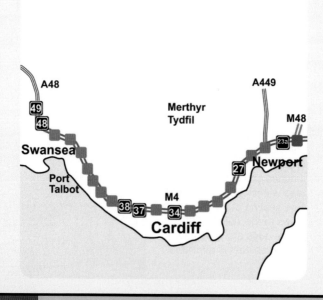

A slightly complicated junction. The approach to the village can confuse the direction to the pub.

 Wheatsheaf
The Square, Magor, S. Wales.
01633 880 608

Satnav
NP26 3HN

Last orders for food: Daily: Noon to 9.30pm.
Sundays: 3.00pm. No evening meals.

                                        ££

Some two hundred
years old, it has a
large modernised
open plan restaurant
and bars where
homemade food is
served.

Take the B4591 road north to Risca and Abertilley. After about 1 mile The Rising Sun is on the left.

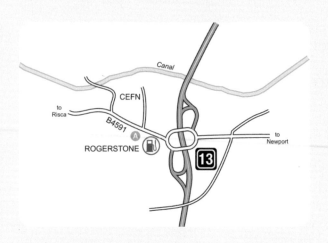

 The Rising Sun

Satnav
NP10 9AQ

1 Cefn Road, Rogerstone, S. Wales
01633 895 126
www.therisingsunnewport.co.uk

Last orders for food: Daily: 2.15pm and 9.30pm.
Sundays: Noon to 8.30pm.

££

A family run pub with a good reputation. It has a two storey conservatory at the rear of the restaurant, with two large bars elsewhere. The menu is imaginative with self-service at lunch. A surprise to find a deservedly popular place which looks unassuming at first sight.

From the junction, take the A4119 towards Llantrisant. A mile down the road, there is a turning to the right to Groesfaen. The Castell Mynach is by the turning.

MISKIN

Castell Mynach ★

Satnav
CF72 8NH

Llantrisant Road, Groesfaen, Pontyclun
01443 237 395

Last orders for food: Mondays to Saturdays: Noon to 10.00pm. Sundays: Noon to 9.30pm.

A busy, cheerful group style pub which has outgrown its origins as a private house. A good atmosphere however and well managed. A girl having a cigarette outside told me it was advisable to book.

At Junction 37 take the short dual carriageway south. At the T-junction turn left. After the roundabout turn right. Over the heathland and follow the signs (now in Welsh) to Kenfig. The easier option is to come off at 38 onto the A48 to Pyle and turn right after a mile. Go under the railway line and right again to Mawdlam and Kenfig. If the Prince of Wales is full the Angel in Mawdlam will look after you.

Places of interest

Margam Abbey(1147). Margam Orangery (1790), the longest in the UK.

Ⓐ **Prince of Wales** ★

Satnav
CF33 4PR

Ton Kenfig. Nr Porthcawl. Mid Glam.
01656 740 356
www.princeofwaleskenfig.com

Last orders for food: Weekdays: 2.30pm and 8.30pm. Sundays: 2.45pm. Mondays: No meals.

 £

A plain-looking building but with a fascinating past. It is a 16th century family owned pub which has a been a

mortuary for shipwrecked bodies. It was also the old Parliament and Court House for the now lost port of Kenfig which was swept away by a tsunami in 1550. It is reputed to be the most haunted pub in Wales but it is however a very friendly pub with a warm welcome.

You can either come off at Junction 48 and after Hendy and the outskirts of Pontardulais turn left on the A48 to Fforest, or else take the simpler option and exit at Junction 49 and take the A48 south. The Bird in Hand will be on your left before Fforest.

 Bird In Hand ★
24 Camarthen Road, Fforest
01792 771 302
www.thebirdinhandswansea.co.uk

Satnav
SA4 0TU

Last orders for food: Weekdays: Noon to 7.45pm. Sundays: Noon to 4.00pm

 £

It is now a managed house of Mitchells and Butler but for the better according to a "regular". It is on the main road facing onto the hills with a row of terraced houses up the hill to the rear. A long dining room has been added so room for all as well as the bar area. A community pub with a cheerful atmosphere and the natives are friendly.

JUNCTIONS **1** TO **31**

The M5 is 168 miles in length and was built in sections, the first part being completed in 1969 and the last in 1976. It was designed to link the Midlands with the South West via Bristol. It is one of the few Motorways which has no connection with London. Considering that it passes through some of the prettiest of the English countryside, the needs of motorists are poorly served.

Droitwich to Tewkesbury

JUNCTIONS **1** TO **10**

A boring stretch of motorway until you get to the south of Worcester.

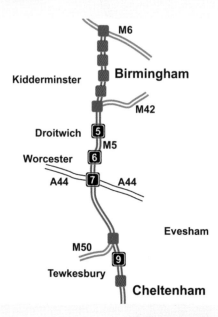

The roundabouts tend to confuse, but look out for the signs to Droitwich

Robin Hood

Rashwood Bank, Rashwood, Worcs.
01527 869 302
www.vintageinns.co.uk/therobinhooddroitwich

Last orders for food: Daily: Noon to 9.30pm.
Saturdays: Noon to 10.00pm.
Sundays: Noon to 9.00pm.

Satnav
WR9 0BS

££

A Mitchell & Butler owned pub with tiled and wooden flooring and a well laid out dining area. It is deservedly well known to the passing motorist. Outside seating and a beer garden at the rear, where dogs are allowed. It has recently been refurbished.

From the junction take the A 4538. Left at the roundabout and after a mile cross over the railway to Crowell Green.

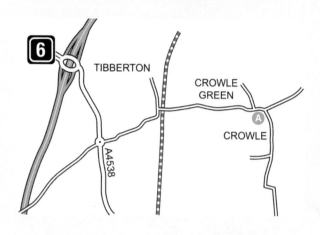

TIBBERTON

CROWLE GREEN

CROWLE

A4538

Ⓐ **Old Chequers** ★

Crowle Green, Crowle, Worcs.
01905 381 275
www.oldchequersinn.com

Satnav
WR7 4AA

Last orders for food: Daily: Noon to 9.00pm.
Sundays: 4.00pm, no evening meals.

££

It has had a makeover with flagged and timber floors, leather chairs and beams. Spacious dining room and a large bar area. Friendly service and a large garden for warm days and where you can play boule.

WORCESTER

A440

KEMPSEY

Take the road to Worcester. At the first roundabout turn left. At the next roundabout turn left on the A38 to Tewkesbury. Kempsey is 3 miles distant and the Walter de Cantelupe is on the left. If it is full there is the Talbot opposite.

Places of interest

Kempsey is reputed to be the most flooded village in the country.

The Walter de Canteloupe Inn ★

Main Road, Kempsey, Worcs.
01905 820 572
www.walterdecantelupe.co.uk

Last orders for food: Weekdays: 2.30pm and 9.30pm. Sundays: 3.00pm

Satnav
WR5 3NA

£££

Named after a 13th century Bishop of Worcester this old merchants house under the aegis of the proprietor, who

was trained in France, offers everything that a weary traveller might want. The furnishing is comfortable but one of bedrooms is said to be haunted. In summer they have a Paella party in the walled garden with home produced food and even a local wine.

The Hobnails is about 4 miles from the junction. Take the
A46 towards Evesham. At the roundabout go straight on
towards Stow-on-the-Wold on the B4077. The inn is on
the left after about 2 miles.

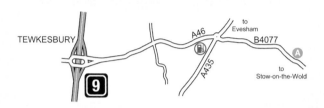

Places of interest
Tewkesbury Abbey (1089)

Ⓐ **Hobnails Inn**
Main Road, Little Washbourne, Glos.
01242 620 237
www.hobnailsinn.co.uk

Satnav
GL20 8NQ

Last orders for food: 2.00pm and 9.00pm.

££

A wayside inn dating back to 1493. It has been refurbished
in a more modern
style with several
small dining areas.
The cooking is tradi-
tional using local
produce and the
carvery is popular.
The service is effi-
cient and friendly
and there is a good
ambience. A garden
for hot weather.

JUNCTIONS 11A TO 21

This stretch takes you from Cheltenham and Gloucester, with its historic cathedral where Edward II is buried, to the south of Bristol. The motorway passes through pleasant countryside and there are interesting houses and places to visit along the River Severn. Near Junction 18, Kings Weston House designed by Sir John Vanbrugh, can be seen on the hills to the east. You can divert along the Avon Gorge into Bristol with its restored dockside and where SS Great Britain is dry docked, after being brought back from the Falklands in 1970 and restored.

During the summer the stretch south from the M4 intersection to the bridge over the Avon can get gridlocked.

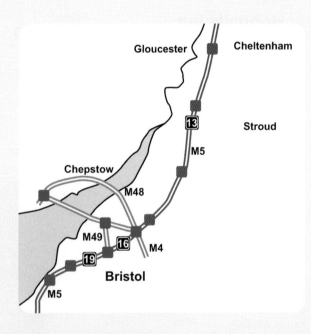

For the Bell take the A38 towards Bristol. After 1 mile turn right to Frampton on Severn. The inn is on the edge of the village green.

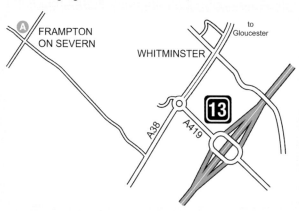

The Bell Inn

The Green, Frampton on Severn, Glos.
01452 740 346
www.thebellatframpton.co.uk

Satnav
GL2 7EP

Last orders for food: Weekdays: 2.30pm and 9.00pm. Fridays, Saturdays and Sundays: Noon to 9.00pm

££

An old coaching inn from the 1700s which has been refurbished. There is a dining room, a bar, log fires in the winter and a friendly reception. Bar meals are served as well as lunches and dinners, morning coffee and afternoon teas. The Bell is at the end of the longest village green in England, with unspoilt examples of Georgian architecture.

Take the A38 to Thornbury, which is dual carriageway. After about ½ mile turn left to Almondsbury opposite the Swan Inn on the right, bear left down the hill and then a sharp right before the Garden Centre. Head for the church next door.

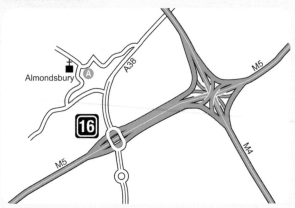

Ⓐ **The Bowl Inn**

Church Road, Lower Almondsbury, S. Glos.
01454 612 157
www.thebowlinn.co.uk

Satnav **BS32 4DT**

Last orders for food: Daily: 2.30pm and 9.45pm. Sundays: Noon to 7.45pm.

                            £££

A privately owned village inn with a restaurant and individually furnished bedrooms under the beamed roof.

The original cottages were built in 1146 to house the builders of the church and it is now a friendly, efficient hostelry with a good menu and service. For those in a hurry such as myself, bar meals are available as well as admiring the view over the River Severn to Wales. It has changed hands.

Take the A369 eastwards but immediately take the road signed Portbury. Keep straight on through the village and follow signs to Clapton in Gordano. In the village, a sharp left up a lane and the pub is on the right,

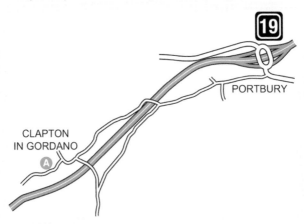

 The Black Horse ★ Satnav **BS20 7RH**
Clevedon Lane, Clapton in Gordano, Som.
01275 842 105
www.thekicker.co.uk

Last orders for food: Weekdays: 2.00pm and 9.00pm. Sundays: 4.00pm.

£

A charming old fashioned pub serving bar meals such as bowls of home made soup, as opposed to a full blown meal. A large garden at the rear where children are welcome. Inside low beams and snugs with flagstone floors. A cheerful and bustling atmosphere and frequented by the locals.

JUNCTIONS **21** TO **31**

South of Bristol the motorway winds over the Mendip Hills before crossing the flat levels of Sedgemoor, remembered for the defeat of the Duke of Monmouth and the Bloody Assizes of "Hanging" Judge Jeffreys.

Glastonbury, famous for the supposed site of the Holy Grail and also for the annual music festival, is close to the motorway.

Taunton is an attractive county town, with a good antique market. The motorway ends south of Exeter which was once a Roman city with a fine medieval cathedral. It continues as dual carriageway to Plymouth and Cornwall.

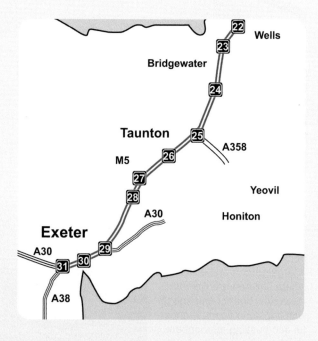

Driving south it is relatively simple. Stay on the A38. The White Cottage is on the left at the end of the village.

Going north, come off at Junction 23 and drive up the A38.

HIGHBRIDGE

HUNTSPILL

R Huntspill

WEST HUNTSPILL

The White Cottage ★

Satnav
TA9 3RQ

Old Pawlett Road, West Huntspill, Som.
01278 794 692

Last orders for food: Weekdays: 1.45pm and 8.45pm. Sundays: 1.30pm and 8.30pm. Monday and Tuesday evenings: Closed.

£

A privately owned restaurant as opposed to a pub so no noisy background, but low beamed with old fashioned charm and a helpful and friendly staff. They were very busy when I passed by but the soup was good and home made. A garden but no out-side meals.

The Puriton Inn is signed just off the junction on the left.

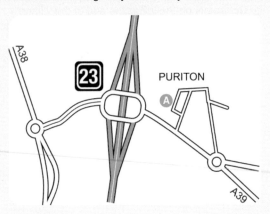

Puriton Inn

Puriton Hill, Puriton, Som
01278 683 464

Satnav
TA7 8AF

Last orders for food: Daily: 2.30pm and 9.30pm.
Sundays: 9.00pm

££

A 200 year old village pub just off the motorway. Dining areas and two bars serving Real Ales. It takes pride in its home cooking. There is a children's playground and outside seating, where dogs are permitted.

This is one of the easiest places to find. Off the motorway to the roundabout on the A38 and the Compass Inn is just 100 yards south. There is a Filling Station on the roundabout.

The Compass Tavern

Satnav
TA6 6PR

Taunton Road, North Petherton, Som.
01278 662 283

Last orders for food: Daily: 3.00pm and 9.00pm.
Sundays: Noon to 9.00pm.

£

A converted 16th century mock Tudor building, with large open beamed dining areas, but pay heed to the notices to "Mind your step or mind your head". Friendly atmosphere with home cooked meals and real Ales. A beer garden where dogs are welcome.

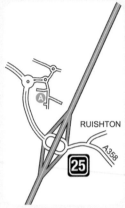

RUISHTON

25

At the junction head towards Taunton. At the first roundabout go right. Right again at the next one and again right at the next. The Hankridge Arms will be on the right surrounded by super-markets.

Places of interest

Hestercombe Gardens (1750's and Gertrude Jekyll)
HHH – 5 miles

The Hankridge Arms

Satnav
TA1 2LR

Hankridge Way, Taunton, Som.
01823 444 405
Last orders for food: Daily: 2.30pm and 9.30pm.
Sundays: Noon to 8.00pm.

 £££

Now a restaurant with a bar area, it was once an Elizabethan farmhouse of some importance, rescued from dereliction by the Hall & Woodhouse Brewery at some considerable cost. No sooner was it completed than it was surrounded by a shopping precinct. It is however a comfortable and friendly place.

Take the minor road to Ford Street. Up the escarpment and to a cross roads. Turn left signed Forches Corner and Holthan Clavel. The inn is about two miles on the right.

Places of interest

Cothay Manor Gardens(1480) HHA

 The Merry Harriers ★ Satnav
EX15 3TR

Forches Corner, Clayhidon. Devon
01823 421 270
www.merryharriers.co.uk

Last orders for food: Weekdays: 3.00pm and 9.00pm. Sundays: 3.00pm. Mondays: Closed

££

An old coaching inn which stands where highwaymen once held sway. The greeting is much friendlier now with low beams and inglenook fires adding to its character. Fresh fish from Brixham and local meat is on the menu and an array of local beers on tap served by a friendly staff. In summer there is a shaded garden.

Getting there is easy enough, but the return is more difficult with what seems to be a needlessly complicated system of roundabouts.

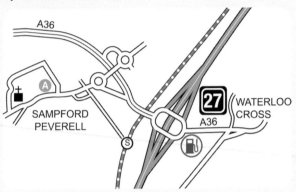

Places of interest
Knightshayes Court (1874) NT – 6 miles

The Globe Inn

Satnav
EX16 7BJ

Lower Town, Sampford Peverell, Devon
01884 821 214
www.globe-in.com
Last orders for food: Daily: 2.30pm and 9.00pm.
Sundays: Noon to 9.00pm.

££

A popular pub with a dining area and bars as well as six double bedrooms. A children's playgound and a beer garden at the rear. Dogs are welcome and there are facilities for the disabled. A skittle alley for use on wet days.

Take the A373 signed Honiton. After about five miles turn left to Broadhembury.

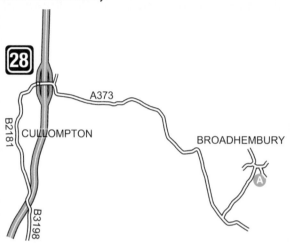

 The Drewe Arms
Main Street, Broadhembury, Devon
01404 841 267
www.thedrewearms.com

Satnav
EX14 3NF

Last orders for food: Weekdays: 3.00pm and 9.00pm. Sundays: 3.00pm. Mondays: Closed

££

The Drewe Arms was built in the 13th century in this attractive estate village. Little seems to have changed and the linenfold panelling and hearths are still there. The welcome from the new owners is as warm as the open fires. The bar has been enlarged and there is a separate dining area. A large garden at the rear where children can play.

Take the A30 to Honiton. After half a mile turn left and pass Clyst Hinton and Exeter Airport, where there is an interesting collection of parked aircraft. Keep on this road for about three miles to Jack-in-the Green and the pub will be on the left.

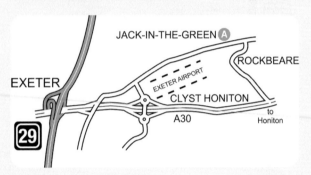

Jack in the Green Inn

Satnav
EX5 2EE

Main Road, Rockbeare, Devon
01404 822 240
www.jackinthegreen.uk.com

Last orders for food: Daily: 2.00pm and 9.00pm.
Sundays: Noon to 9.00pm

££

The inn has been there for several centuries and has

been modernised with a lounge bar and a restaurant in the old part. Leather sofas in the sitting areas and out-side seating in an enlarged patio for summer days. It is the venue for the local hot air balloon club for those want-ing an uplifting experience!

For the Blue Ball – up to the first roundabout to return and take the first left. From there, continue on the minor road into Topsham. Head for Ebford and the Bridge Inn is on the left. For the Digger's Rest go to Clyst St. George – then on to the B3179 to Woodbury and second left to Woodbury Salterton.

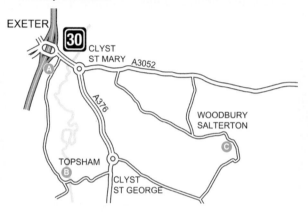

Ⓐ **Blue Ball Inn**

Clyst Road, Sandygate, Devon
01392 873 401

www.theblueballpub.com

Last orders for food: Daily: 2.30pm and 9.30pm.
Sundays: Noon to 9.00pm.

Satnav
EX2 7JL

££

An attractive 18th Century pub cum restaurant in a quiet lane. Scrubbed tables, tiled floors, low beamed ceilings and home cooking give a homely feeling. Coffee and teas can also be had. There is a large garden, but dogs are not particularly welcomed.

ⓑ The Bridge Inn

Satnav
EX3 0QQ

Bridge Hill, Topsham, Devon
01392 873 862
www.chessers.co.uk

Last orders for food: Daily: Lunches only until 2.00pm. No evening meals.

 £

This Inn has character in spades and dates back to the

 16th century. It has been in the same family ownership since 1897 and it is known throughout the South West for its Real Ales. It serves good traditional bar lunches. Children and dogs are welcome. Outside seating by a weir on the River Clyst. (Another accolade is that the Queen paid an official visit there in 1998.)

ⓒ Digger's Rest

Satnav
EX5 1PQ

Main Road, Woodbury Salterton, Devon
01395 232 375
www.diggersrest.co.uk

Last orders for food: 2.00pm and 9.00pm.

 ££

A fifty year old cider house, now a pub cum restaurant in

 the centre of the village with a thatched roof, low beams and a cheerful fire. The name derives from an Australian who owned it for a year some forty years ago, but the name remains. What also remains is the good cooking, efficient service and, depending on who is serving, a reminder of its Australian antecedents.

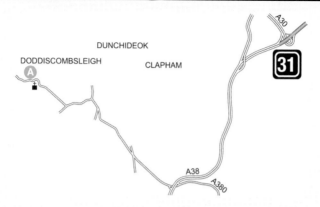

The Nobody Inn is 4 miles from the A38 Exeter Race Course road. The last part is through narrow Devon lanes but worth the journey.

 **Nobody Inn** ★
Main Road, Doddiscombsleigh, Devon
01647 252 394
www.nobodyinn.co.uk

Satnav
EX6 7PS

Last orders for food: 2.15pm and 9.00pm.
Sundays: Noon to 7.00pm.

£££

This could be deemed the lollipop of the M5 towards the end of what could be a tedious journey on a hot summers day. Tucked away in deep countryside it has a large bar for lunches and a restaurant for evening meals where the renowned wine cellar can be fully appreciated. Privately owned it ensures a good menu and a friendly service.

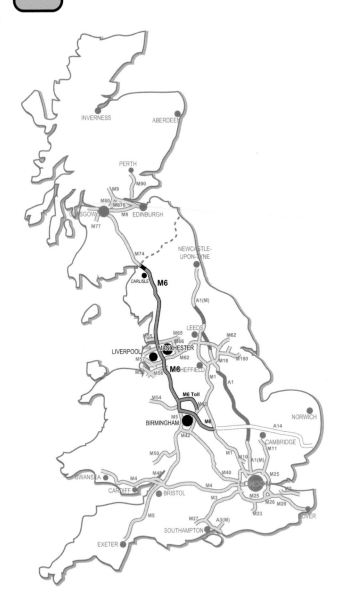

JUNCTIONS **T1** TO **11A**

This is the latest addition to the motorway network and was opened in 2004, apparently using pulped old books to strengthen it.

Built by private enterprise under the aegis of the then government, it has certainly improved those endless traffic jams at Spaghetti Junction which added hours to journey times, but you must pay for this advantage. You will also have to pay to regain the motorway after having a meal, so I have decided to omit any entries there may be.

JUNCTIONS 1 TO 44

The first trial section of a motorway was built as the Preston Bypass in 1958, before the M1 was finished in 1959. The M6 is one of the longest motorways, being some 180 miles in length. It was built over a period of years, starting in 1962 and the last section was finished in 1972. The link over the Scottish Border connecting up with the A74(M) is still being completed to motorway standard.

Rugby to Stafford

JUNCTIONS 1 TO 14

This section of the motorway is dull and when combined with the inevitable snarl up at Spaghetti Junction, it becomes downright tedious. It gets better just south of Stafford. The opening of the new M6(Toll) has improved matters, but I should hurry on as best you can.

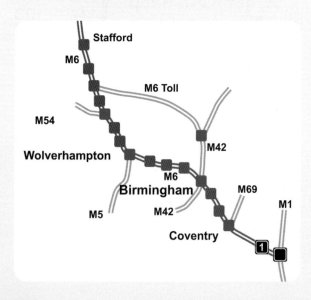

Take the A426 to Rugby. At the first roundabout turn left for 2.5 miles to the A6 (Watling Street). Go right and then left to Catthorpe.

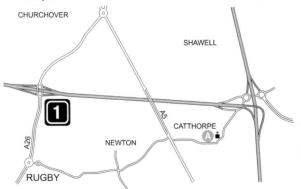

Places of interest
Stanford Hall & Park (1690) HHA – 2 miles.

 ## Manor Farm Shop
Main Street, Catthorpe, Leics.
01788 869 002
www.manorfarmcatthorpe.co.uk

Satnav
LE17 6DB

Last orders for food: Daily: 10.00am to 4.00pm.
Teas to 5.00pm.

£

A genuine working farm which has diversified. In a converted barn there is a Craft Shop and the Tea Room serves morning coffee, light lunches and afternoon teas. There is outside seating and a car park. Dogs and children are welcome.

JUNCTIONS 15 TO 32

Stoke on Trent is the home of pottery, most of which is attractive, but the same could not be said for the town itself. Nearby Barlaston Hall was built in 1756 by the architect Sir Robert Taylor for the Wedgwood family as their home and factory. It was shamefully neglected by the firm, until saved at the last moment by SAVE Britain's Heritage in 1978.

The countryside in Cheshire is pleasant enough, but once over the Manchester Ship Canal, the surroundings are crowded with motorways. It is small wonder that the local inhabitants were beginning to complain as more and more of their land was being taken to build yet another motorway.

Barthomley is 1 mile from the Junction. The White Lion is 200 feet from the church.

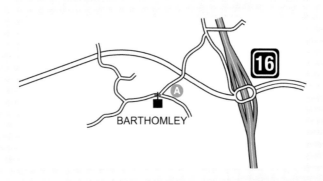

BARTHOMLEY

White Lion Inn ★

Audley Road, Barthomley, Cheshire.
01270 882 242
www.whitelionbartomley.com

Satnav
CW2 5PG

Last orders for food: Weekdays: 2.00pm and 9.00pm. Sundays: 2.30pm.

£££

A Grade 2 listed build-
ing which is an old
fashioned tavern with a
bar in one room and an
inglenook fire in the
other. It was built in
1614 and has not
changed all that much
since then.

Take the A534 to Congleton. Almost immediately turn left on the A5022 signed Brereton Green. The Bears Head is on the far side of the village.

Places of interest

Little Moreton Hall(1504-1610) NT – 6 miles.

(A) **Bears Head Hotel** ★

Satnav
CW11 1RS

Newcastle Road South, Brereton, Ches.
01477 544 732
www.vintageinn.co.uk/thebearsheadbrereton

Last orders for food: Weekdays: Noon to 10.00pm. Sundays: Noon to 9.30pm.

 £££

Built in 1625 as the Boars Head. It was a Posting House

on the Post road between London and Liverpool. A new wing and stables were added in the 18th century. It is now a comfortable modern hostelry with all the creature comforts that the hot and tired motorist might need.

No difficulty with this junction.

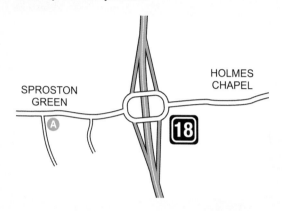

HOLMES
CHAPEL

SPROSTON
GREEN

18

Places of interest
Capesthorne Hall (1719-1837) HHA – 11 miles

Ⓐ Fox and Hounds

Satnav
CW4 7LW

Holmes Chapel Road, Sproston Green, Ches.
01606 832 303

Last orders for food: Daily: 2.30pm and 9.00pm.
Summer: 8.00pm. Mondays: No evening meals.

££

A wayside pub still owned by the Punch Group, but for
the past thirteen
years run by the
same people. It
has a dining room
and bars with
flagstone floors
and beamed ceil-
ings. A garden for
children and dogs
are welcome.

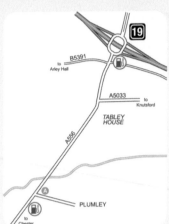

The Smoker at Plumley
may seem to be a bit
far for those in a hurry,
but worth it.

Places of interest

Arley Hall & Gardens (19th C) HHA – 5 miles
Tatton Park 18th & 19th C) NT – 3 miles
Tabley House (18th C) University of Manchester – 2 miles

 The Smoker

Chester Road, Plumley, Ches.
01565 722 338
www.thesmokerinn.co.uk

Satnav
WA16 0TY

Last orders for food: Daily: 2.15pm and 9.15pm.
Sundays: Noon to 9.00pm.

££

A well known hostelry which
has been modernised into a
comfortable restaurant and a
bar area with an imaginative
menu. For those in a hurry
there is a sandwich menu. In
addition there is a large garden, open fires and plenty of
seating. You will have to ask
why it is called The Smoker.

From Junction 27 take the B5250 towards Eccleston. Wrightington Bar is 2.5 miles along this road. The Mulberry Tree is at the apex of a fork in the road at the end of the village.

The Mulberry Tree

Satnav
WN6 9SE

9 Wood Lane, Wrightington Bar, Lancs.
01257 451 400
www.themulberrytree.info

Last orders for food: Daily: 2.30pm and 9.30pm.
Saturday and Sunday: Noon to 9.30pm.

£££

A privately owned Bar, Restaurant and Country Bar. It has been modernised to form a large open eating area by the bar and there is a separate restaurant. Traditional British cooking with a twist as described to me. Efficient service and a pleasant change.

Not an easy junction. Turn right at the traffic lights and
bear right at the village green.

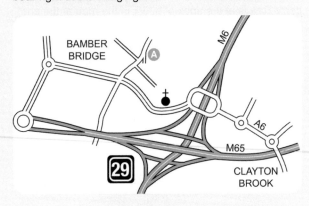

Ye Olde Hob Inn

Satnav
PR5 6EP

Church Road, Bamber Bridge, Lancs.
01772 336 863

Last orders for food: Daily: 2.00pm and 9.00pm.
Mondays, Tuesdays and Sundays: 8.00pm.

   £

A welcome surprise to find an old rustic, thatched roof,

traditional pub, al-
though it is owned
by Scottish and
Newcastle. It has
a restaurant as
well as a bar, with
outside seating
and a family room
for wet weather.

JUNCTIONS 33 TO 44

This section is the most scenic of any of the motorways. After Lancaster, which is an interesting county town, the motorway climbs up past Kendal with views of the Lake District to the west and the Pennines to the east. Once over Shap the highest point of the motorway, it descends past Penrith, a picturesque market town to the south of Carlisle which is well worth a visit. From there the motorway crosses over the River Esk into Scotland.

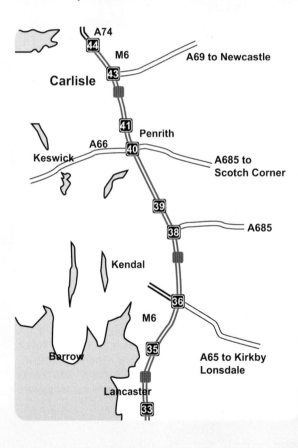

From the junction drive into Broughton. At the crossroads turn right to Goosnargh on the B5269. The Italian Orchard is on the right just before you go under the motorway.

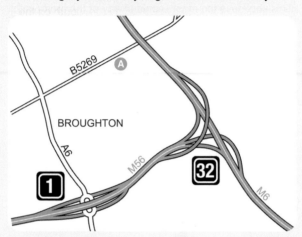

 **Italian Orchard** ★

Satnav
PR3 5DB

Whittingham Lane, Broughton, Lancs.
01772 861 240
www.oldchequersinn.com

Last orders for food: Weekdays: 3.00pm and 9.00pm. Sundays: Noon to 9.00pm.

£££

No prizes for guessing the sort of ambiance you will find. Need I say more. However, it is extremely modern and comfortable, with a high standard, and not for those in a hurry.

GALGATE

33

to
Garstand

The Canalside Craft Centre is
on the left when you come
into Galgate. For The Bay
Horse Inn turn south on the
A6 and it will be brown
signed to the left.

 Canalside Craft Centre

Satnav
LA2 0LQ

Main Road, Galgate, Lancs.
01524 752 223
Last orders for food: Daily: 3.00pm (winter),
4.00pm (summer). Mondays: Closed.

£

A craft centre with a
coffee shop serving
everything from toast
to a full meal.
An ideal spot for
those just wanting a
light lunch and an air-
ing for dogs or chil-
dren along the canal
bank. Home made
meals, soups and
cakes a speciality.

For the Bay Horse turn left at the roundabout on the A6 towards Garstang. After 400 yards bear left, where it is browned signed to the Bay Horse for a mile. Coming from the south at Potters Brook bear right as signed.

The Bay Horse Inn

Satnav
LA2 0HR

Bay Horse Lane, Forton, Lancs.
01524 791 204

www.bayhorseinn.com

Last orders for food: Daily: 2.00pm and 9.15pm.
Sundays: 3.00pm.

££

It is a secluded 18th century pub cum restaurant down a quiet country lane. It has a well deserved reputation for food and a friendly ambiance with a cheerful bar, log fires an a separate dining room.

Over Kellet with its village green and rural post office is easy to find. Those of us old enough to remember seeing "Brief Encounter" can go and see where it was filmed in Carnforth Station.

Places of interest
Leighton Hall (1246 – 19th C) HHA – 3 miles

The Eagles Head

Satnav
LA6 1DL

Main Street, Over Kellet, Lancs.
01524 732 457

Last orders for food: Daily: 2.30pm and 9.00pm.
Saturday and Sunday: Noon to 9.00pm.

£

A cheerful country pub where bar meals are served daily in a large dining area cum bar with exposed stone walls and timber ceilings. It specialises in home cured and cooked ham. It has recently changed hands.

A boring junction with dual carriageways on either side.
Look out for the Crooklands Hotel signs.

Places of interest
Levens Hall (16th C) Gardens (1614) HHA – 4 miles
Sizergh Castle (14th & 16th C) NT – 5 miles

Ⓐ Crooklands Hotel

Satnav
LA7 7NW

Crooklands, Lancs.
01539 567 432
www.crooklands.com

Last orders for food: Daily: 2.00pm and 9.00pm.

 **££/£££**

A comfortable privately
owned hotel with 30 double
rooms in a new extension. It
has a restaurant as well as a
carvery and bars also serving
meals. Morning coffee for the
passing motorist. Children,
but no dogs.

Dual carriageways lead off and onto the motorway. At the roundabout take the B6260 on the left signed Orton. The George is in the village and on the left. Another good reason to stop in Orton is the famous Kennedys chocolate factory which is on the other side of the road where you can buy something for the journey or as a present.

Places of interest
The Roman fort and road at Low Borrowbridge - 3miles

George Hotel ★

Front Street, Orton, Cumbria.
015396 242 229
www.thegeorgehotelorton.co.uk

Satnav
CA10 3JR

Last orders for food: Daily: 2.30pm and 9.00pm.
Sundays: Noon to 9.00pm.

Not really a hotel but more of a locals bar with stone flagged floors and scrubbed tables. However it is friendly place and the staff are helpful. Dogs and children are welcome.

An easy junction.
Picnics on a fine day.

Places of interest
Shap Abbey (EH) – 3 miles

 The Greyhound Hotel Satnav
CA10 3PW
Main Street, Shap, Cumbria
01931 716 474
www.greyhoundshap.co.uk

Last orders for food: Daily: 2.00pm and 9.00pm.
Sundays: 2.30pm and 9.00pm.

Apparently Bonnie Prince Charlie spent a night on his

way south in 1745.
It has been taken
over by the previ-
ous lessee of the
Cross Keys in
Tebay. It serves
good local lamb
and fresh fish. For
those spending the
night beware of the
main railway just
behind.

For the Gate Inn take the road to Eamont Bridge and turn right on the Tirril road for one mile. For the others take the A66 to Keswick. Left at the first roundabout on the A592 and right to Stainton. The Brantwood Hotel is on the right and the Kings Arms to the left.

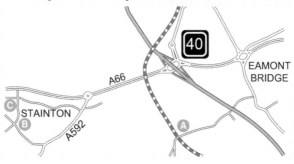

Places of interest
Dalemain (15th C and 19th C)
The Toffee Shop, Penrith

The Gate Inn

Satnav
CA10 2LF

Old Road, Yarnworth, Cumbria
01768 862 386
www.yanwathgate.com

Last orders for food: Daily: 2.30pm and 9.00pm.

££

A privately owned pub dating from 1683, which was originally a toll gate, in a quiet secluded lane with whitewashed exposed stone walls. It has a dining room and bar, as well as outside seating. The sign over the door says "This gate hangs well and hinders none. Refresh and pay and travel on".

Kings Arms

Satnav
CA11 0EP

The Green, Stainton, Cumbria
01768 862 778

Last orders for food: Daily: 2.00pm and 9.00pm.
Sundays: Noon to 9.00pm.

       ££

The new owners of this
18th Century rural pub
provide an extensive
menu of homemade
and vegetable dishes.
Friendly welcome and
you get what you see.
Outside seating on hot
days and dogs are
welcome.

Brantwood Country Hotel Satnav
CA11 0EP

Main Street, Stainton, Cumbria
01768 862 748
www.brantwoodhotel.co.uk

Last orders for food: Weekdays: 2.15pm and
9.30pm. Sundays: 8.30pm.

       £££

A family owned hotel and
restaurant with a large garden. A comfortably furnished
house with oak beams and
log fires.

From the Junction take the B5305. Straight on at the roundabout signed Lazonby. Left at the T-junction. Right at the first crossroads into Great Salkeld and head for the church. 100 yards on the right is the pub.

Places of interest

Hutton-in-the-Forest. (15c to 19 c) HHA   3miles.

 **Highland Drove** ★

Satnav
CA11 9NA

Main Street, Great Salkeld, Cumbria
01768 898 349
www.highland-drove.co.uk

Last orders for food: Daily: 2.00pm and 9.00pm.
Sundays: Noon to 9.00pm. Mondays: No lunches.

££

The building dates back a few hundred years and still serves the needs of the local community and now the passing motorist. Father and son Newton have ensured an enduring standard of a good atmosphere and of cooking using local produce.

For the Crown Hotel take the road to Wetheral, which is 2 miles from the junction. At the village green turn left.

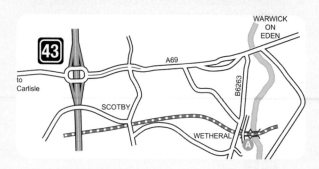

Places of interest
Carlisle Castle and Cathedral

Ⓐ **Crown Hotel**

Station Road, Wetheral, Cumbria
01228 561 888
www.thecrownhotelwetheral.co.uk

Satnav
CA4 8ES

Last orders for food: Daily: 2.00pm and 9.00pm.

££/£££

The Crown Hotel dates back to the old coaching days

and is now a modern and efficient country hotel. Waltons Bar is an ideal place for a quick meal with a friendly welcome. A large garden for fresh air and an in-door swimming pool.

At the junction take the A689 signed Brampton and left at the roundabout. After 1.5 miles bear right into the village and then follow the signs.

Places of interest
Hadrians Wall (Turf)

 ## Crosby Lodge Hotel ★
High Crosby, Crosby on Eden, Cumbria
01228 573 618
www.crosbylodge.co.uk

Satnav
CA6 4QZ

Last orders for food: Daily: 2.30pm and 9.00pm.

£££

It was built as a country mansion in 1805 overlooking spacious gardens with parkland and the River Eden. In 1970 the Sedgwick family bought it and converted it into an hotel with character and a collection of Victorian settees. Meals in the grand dining room but bar meals are available for those in a hurry. Dogs by arrangement. It could be the required lollipop for those after a long car journey from the south.

JUNCTIONS 7 TO 14

For those travelling to or from the Channel Tunnel it is a good alternative to the M1 as it links the M25 with the A1(M) at Huntingdon

The southern section goes past the town of Harlow and the congestion around Stansted Airport. Once north of them, the countryside is pleasant enough and passes some attractive towns such as Saffron Walden and the imposing pile of Audley End. At Duxford is the American Air Museum and the Imperial War Museum. Cambridge of course is a must for anyone who has never been there.

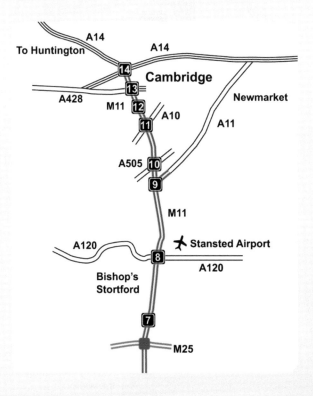

 M11 | **7** Harlow A414 Chelmsford

The roundabout is controlled by lights. Take the Chelmsford road and almost immediately turn off to the left on a small road which is marked St. Clare Hospice and Hastingwood.

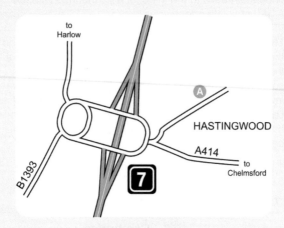

 The Rainbow and Dove Satnav **CM17 9JX**
Hastingwood Road, Hastingwood, Essex
01279 415 419

Last orders for food: Daily: 2.30pm and 9.30pm.
Sundays: 3.00pm.

£

Now a free house which is a rural pub cum restaurant.

It is said to date from the 15th century and was certainly a pub in 1645, when Cromwell's soldiers stopped there. There is outside seating in a garden and inside a roaring fire during the winter.

Construction work has been completed to cope with the increasing traffic to and from Stansted Airport. Keep going around the roundabout until you see the small turnoff for Birchanger.

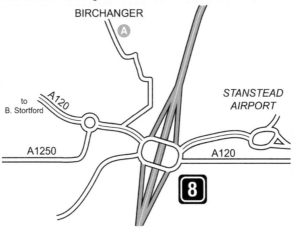

 The Three Willows

Birchanger Lane, Birchanger, Herts.
01279 815 913

Satnav
CM23 5QL

Last orders for food: Daily: 2.00pm and 9.00pm.
Sundays: 2.00pm.

££

A popular restaurant-cum-pub, with a strong cricket influence judging by the inn sign outside and indoors as part has been designated The Oval. It specialises in fish and there are also bar meals. There is a children's playground, where they are meant to stay.

This junction gives direct access to the Newmarket road.
Then bear left where marked Great Chesterford. If driving north, you must access again at Junction 10 and vice versa.

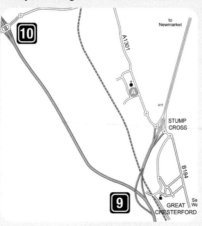

Places of interest

Audley End House (Jacobean) EH – 5 miles

 ## The Red Lion

High Street, Hinxton, Cambs.
01799 530 601
www.redlionhinxton.co.uk

Satnav
CB10 1QY

Last orders for food: Daily: 2.00pm and 9.00pm.
Fridays and Saturdays: 2.00pm and 9.30pm.
Sundays: 2.30pm and 9.30pm.

    ££

A 16th century pub in this attractive village. A well deserved reputation for home cooking in the restaurant and bar. Friendly atmosphere and a warm welcome.

Take the A505 to Royston. A mile after the Imperial War
Museum, turn right to Thriplow. Left at the T-Junction in
the village.

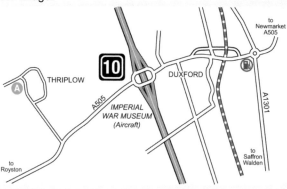

Places of interest

The Imperial War Museum and American Air Museum.

 # The Green Man ★

Lower Street, Thriplow, Herts.

01763 208 855

www.greenmanatthriplow.co.uk

Satnav
SG8 7RJ

Last orders for food: Daily: 2.30pm and 9.00pm.
Sundays: Noon to 9.00pm

 £

Very much a pub serving rea-
sonably priced meals from a
simple menu. There are no
fruit machines, juke boxes or
piped music which makes for
a more peaceful rest. The ex-
terior has been painted blue,
to make a change from
green? The interior has also
had a facelift.

M11 | **11** Cambridge (South) A1309
Royston, Harston A10

From the junction take the A10 to Royston. After about half a mile turn left onto the B1368 to Newton. The Queen's Head is on the other side of the village green.

Queens Head

Fowlhers Road, Newton, Cambs.
01223 870 436

Satnav
CB22 7PG

Last orders for food: Daily: 2.15pm and 9.30pm.
Sundays: 2.15pm and 9.00pm.

££

A pleasant and friendly hostelry with well furnished dining alcoves and bars and a host of interesting mementos. Good food and a warm welcome – what more could you need.

166   M11 London to Cambridge

The picturesque village of Grantchester was made famous by the First World War poet, Rupert Brooke, "… Is there honey still for tea?"

Places of interest
Wimpole Hall (18th C Style) NT – 6 miles

The Rupert Brooke

Satnav
CB3 9NQ

Broadway, Grantchester, Cambs.
01223 840 295
www.therupertbrooke.com

Last orders for food: Daily: 2.45pm and 9.15pm.
Sundays: No evening meals.

££

Converted from a 19th century house into a privately owned restaurant with bar areas, which is due to be modernised again. A garden at the rear, overlooking the meadows.

B **The Green Man**
High Street, Grantchester, Cambs.
01223 844 669
www.thegreenmangrantchester.co.uk

Satnav
CB3 9NF

Last orders for food: Mondays to Thursdays:
2.30pm and 9.00pm. Fridays, Saturdays and
Sundays: 3.00pm and 10.00pm.

 £

A traditional pub in the centre of the village since 1510, which has been renovated with wooden floors and a bar. A garden at the rear and fires in the winter.

C **The Orchard**
Millway, Grantchester, Cambs.
01223 845 788
www.orchard-grantchester.com

Satnav
CB3 7BG

Last orders for food: Daily: 9.30am and 5.30pm.
Summer: 9.30am and 7.00pm

 ££

Now over 100 years old, it is still an old fashioned tea

room complete with 1920s deckchairs, punts and nostalgia. You almost expect to see previous visitors such as Rupert Brooke, Virginia Woolfe, A.A. Milne or John Betjeman appear from behind an apple tree. Light lunches available as well as traditional teas in and out of doors depending on the weather.

Junction 13 is easy for those coming from the south, but junction 14, for those coming from the north, will require a degree of map reading. However, it is well worth the effort to get to Madingley.

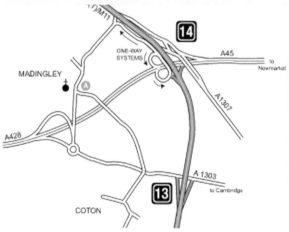

Ⓐ **The Three Horseshoes**

Satnav
CB3 8AB

High Street, Madingley, Cambs.
01954 210 221
www.threehorseshoesmadingly.co.uk

Last orders for food: Daily: 2.00pm and 9.00pm.
Sundays: 2.30pm and 8.30pm.

£££

Part of a small group of well managed pub/restaurants run by chefs. Inside there is a restaurant and long bar, with a conservatory at the rear. Outside there is a pleasant garden.

JUNCTIONS **1** TO **7**

This 30 mile motorway was built to link the M1 to the A1(M) at Doncaster, then with the M180 spur to Grimsby and finally with the M62 Trans Penine near Goole. It is a useful linking motorway as you can switch from the M1 or else cut off a corner when travelling to or from Hull. That being said, the countryside is flat and uninteresting. Selby however, to the north of the intersection with M62, is worth a visit, as the abbey was built at the same time and probably by the same masons as Durham Cathedral.

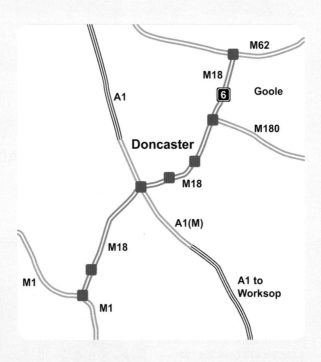

This is an area of low fen land and irrigation ditches.

Waterside, where canal boats once disgorged their cargoes, was renowned for having seven pubs but only one now remains. It is said that an Elizabethan warship was built here to harrass the Armada.

Places of interest

The birthplace of Thomas Crapper, the manufacturer of flushing lavatories

 ## The John Bull Inn

Waterside, Doncaster
01788 860 318
www.chequersswinford.co.uk

Satnav
DN8 4JQ

Last orders for food: Daily: Not applicable for the time being.

                                             £

A traditional inn, by the canal, where ale has been served to thirsty bargemen since 1500's. The kitchen is being rebuilt, so no food will be available for the forseeable future. Comments please.

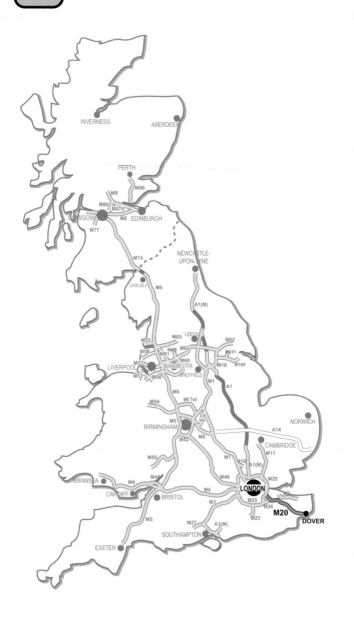

JUNCTIONS 1 TO 13

The M20 is 40 miles long and was started in 1961 and finished twenty years later. It is the main motorway from the Channel Ports to link up directly with the M25 and the entire motorway system.

It goes through some very attractive scenery, known as the Garden of England. There are proposals to submerge the area with new houses, so enjoy it whilst you can.

After Maidstone, with its orchards and oast houses, the M20 climbs the shoulder of the North Weald on its way to London, whilst the M26 spur continues and links up with the southern segment of the M25.

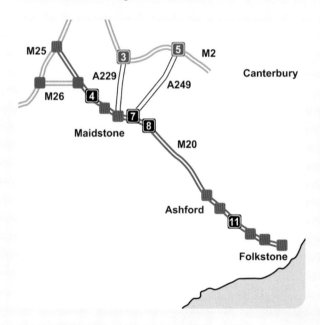

It seems a long way from the junction, but worth the journey.

The Angel Inn

Main Street, Addington Green, Kent
01732 842 117
www.theangelinnaddington.co.uk

Satnav
ME19 5BB

Last orders for food: Daily: 2.00pm and 9.30pm.
Sundays: Noon to 8.30pm.

An atmospheric 14th Century inn with low beams, log fires and garlands of dried hops. Meals are served on hewn wooden tables in areas divided by posts. There is a restaurant in the adjoining converted stables. A large garden and meals can be taken under a pergola.

This junction is close to Maidstone and therefore it is a more built up area. The Eurostar railtrack makes it more confusing.

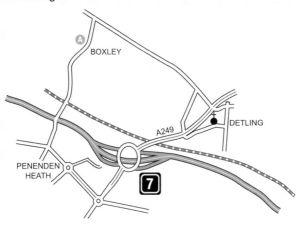

 Kings Arms

The Street, Boxley, Kent
01622 755 177

Satnav
ME13 3DR

Last orders for food: Daily: 2.30pm and 9.00pm.
Sundays: 3.30pm.

££

A traditional, family run village pub with a cheerful atmosphere, beams and log fires. A separate dining room as well as a bar serving bar meals. A car park opposite and a large garden at the rear with a heated patio. Well behaved dogs and children welcomed.

Not a complicated junction, but look out for the sign to Hollingbourne.

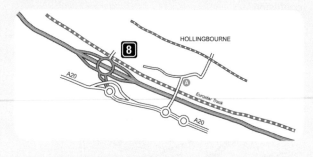

Places of interest

Leeds Castle (Med) Pte – 2 miles
Stoneacre (15th C) NT – 3 miles

 The Windmill
Eythorne Street, Hollingbourne, Kent
01622 880 280
www.windmillkent.com

Satnav
ME17 1TR

Last orders for food: Daily: 2.30pm and 9.30pm.
Weekends: Noon to 9.30pm.

                                          ££

A privately owned pub in an attractive village, which

dates back partially to the 16th Century. It has a dining room and bar serving home cooked meals. Outside there is a children's playground at the rear. It has recently changed hands.

The new Eurostar track now runs alongside the motor-way. Circle round to the north on the B2068 and then left to Stanford (North).

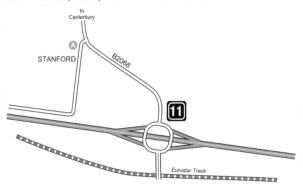

The Drum
Stone Street, Stanford North, Kent
01303 812 125
www.thedruminn.com

Satnav
TN25 6DN

Last orders for food: 2.00pm and 9.00pm.

                                    ££

It is the last hostelry before (or first after) the Tunnel. It has been a country pub for some 300 years and log fires still burn in the grates. There is a dining room and a bar for snacks, home cooking and Real Ales. Outside seating in the garden.

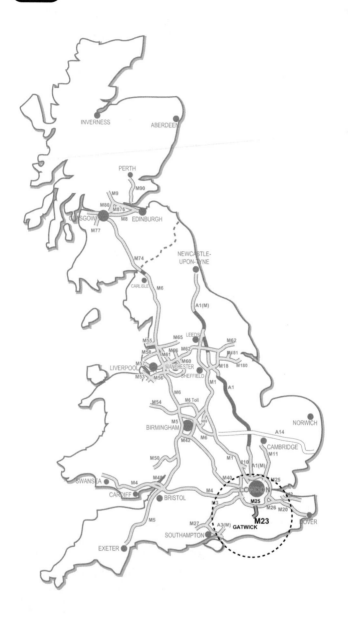

JUNCTIONS **7** TO **11**

Built to give quick access from Gatwick Airport to London via Croydon, this 18 miles stretch took nearly four years to complete. However, the roads south of Croydon are so congested that many motorists prefer to head west to the M25 and then drive round to the M23.

Gatwick Airport started life as a racecourse in the 19th Century before becoming one of the busiest airports in the UK, in spite of only having one runway.

At junction 11 it continues as the A23 to Brighton.

An easy junction's the Hotel is on the other side of the roundabout.

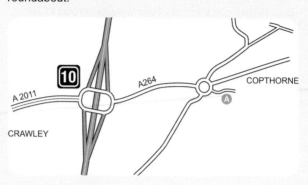

Places of interest
Wakehurst Place, (1590)
Royal Botanic Gardens, Kew – 6 miles

Ⓐ Copthorne Hotel
London Road, Copthorne, W. Sussex
01342 714 971
www.milleniumhotel.co.uk

Satnav
RH10 3PG

Last orders for food: Daily: No lunches,but evening meals until 11.00pm.
Sundays: Lunches only.

£££

It is a large modern hotel catering for businessmen and

travellers. The White Swan is all that is left of the original buildings which has comfortable restaurant style areas. At the moment it does not serve lunches, but dinner until 11.00pm. In the hotel itself, there is a full range of leisure activities.

JUNCTIONS 1A TO 30

The idea of an orbital ring road around London was first mooted in 1905. The North Circular Road was built in the 1930's, but the South Circular exists in name only.

In 1975 a decision was made to construct an integrated Orbital Ring Road, which was finally completed in 1986. It was originally intended to have more lanes, but this was deemed to be too expensive. It will now cost a fortune to upgrade it to cope with the increase in traffic.

The M25 does however, make it easier for visitors from abroad to skirt around London and head north or west.

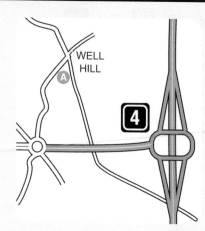

WELL HILL

4

As a junction it is an easy one, but at the roundabout look out for a narrow lane signed Well Hill.

Places of interest

Lullingstone Castle (15th C) HHA – 2 miles
Lullingstone Roman Villa EH – 2 miles

Bo Peep Restaurant

Satnav
BR6 7QL

Hewitts Road, Well Hill, Kent
01959 534 457
www.thebopeep.com

Last orders for food: Daily: 2.00pm and 9.00pm.
Fridays and Saturdays: 2.00pm and 9.30pm.
Sundays: No evening meals.

£

It has been an alehouse since 1549. It is a surprise to find somewhere so close to London and still in the middle of strawberry fields. It has a dining room and a bar for snacks. A well kept garden and inside a friendly welcome.

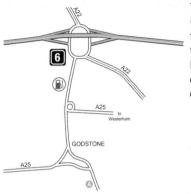

Take the B2236 to Godstone and through this attractive village. The Bell is on the right of the road as you come out.

Places of interest

Chartwell. (Sir Winston Churchill) NT- 8 miles.
Squerryes Court (17c) HHA- 7 miles.
Quebec House (16c) NT- 8 miles

 The Bell Inn ★

Satnav
RH9 8DX

High Street, Godstone, Surrey
01883 743 216
www.thebellgodstone.co.uk

Last orders for food: Daily: 2.30pm and 9.00pm.
Sundays: Noon to 9.00pm.

 ££

It has had a major makeover and is now a cheerful bustling gastro pub with friendly and efficient service.

A fairly tortuous intersection. Head to Uxbridge on the
M40 for 1.5 miles and come off at Junction 1. Go north
on the A413 towards Chalfont St. Giles for 1 mile and
bear right on the A412 to Rickmansworth. After 400
yards turn right to Denham. Returning, go under the
motorway and rejoin the M40 via two roundabouts and
then onto the M25.

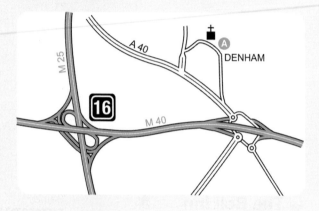

Swan Inn

Village Road, Denham, Bucks.
01895 832 085
www.swaninndenham.co.uk

Satnav
UB9 5BH

Last orders for food: 2.30pm and 10.00pm.
Sundays: 4.00pm and 9.30pm.

  ££

The Swan is much fre-
quented by both locals and
visitors. The cooking is described as British Colonial
which conjures up images of
the Raj. The dining room is
small and cosy and the bar
also serves as a meeting
place. A pleasant garden outside for warm summer days.

At the first crossroads look out for a sign saying Dog Kennel Road. For the Fox and Hounds and Bedford Arms continue through Chorleywood and bear to the right which is signed Chenies.

Places of interest
Chenies Manor House (14th & 15th C) HHA – 3 miles

The Black Horse

Satnav **WD3 5EG**

Dog Kennel Rd,Chorleywood Common,Herts.
01923 282 252

Last orders for food: Daily: 2.15pm and 9.00pm.
Sundays: Noon to 4.00pm. No evening meals.

££

A pub since the early 1800's it now has dining areas and produces home cooked specials by log fires in the restaurant or bar areas. There is a children's menu. Dogs have the freedom of the Common.

ⓑ **Red Lion** ★

Main Road, Chenies, Bucks.
019232 282 722
www.redlionchenies.co.uk

Satnav
WD3 6ED

Last orders for food: Weekdays: 2.00pm and
10.00pm. Sundays: Noon to 9.00pm

 £ £

Once a coaching stop, it is
now a traditional country pub
with no piped music or fruit
machines. It has an imaginative menu and the owners, for
the past twenty years, have
made sure that standards
have been kept. A cheerful
place with friendly staff.

ⓒ **Bedford Arms Hotel** ★

Latimer Road, Chenies, Bucks.
01923 283 301
www.befordarms.co.uk

Satnav
WD3 6EQ

Last orders for food: Weekdays: 2.00pm and
10.00pm. Sundays: Noon to 9.00pm.

 £ £ £

A Georgian house which has
been converted into a comfortable country hotel with a
restaurant and a large garden. A peaceful haven in the
country to recover from the
trauma of the M25.

Take the road towards St Albans but at the first round-about bear left to Chiswell Green and then first left to Potters Crouch The roads are narrow and not helped by the road widening of the M25 and the resultant lorry traffic. Well worth the effort.

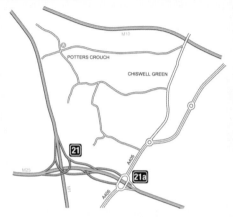

Ⓐ The Holly Bush ★

Satnav
AL2 3NN

Ragged Hall Lane, Potters Crouch, Herts.
01727 851 792
www.thehollybushpub.co.uk

Last orders for food: Daily: 2.00pm and 9.00pm.
Sundays: 2.30pm.

££

A 17th-century country pub covered with wisteria near a rural hamlet. It has been run by the same family for 30years and is filled with old furniture, varnished tables, log fires and a cheerful atmosphere. Outside there is a mature garden for a moment of relaxation.

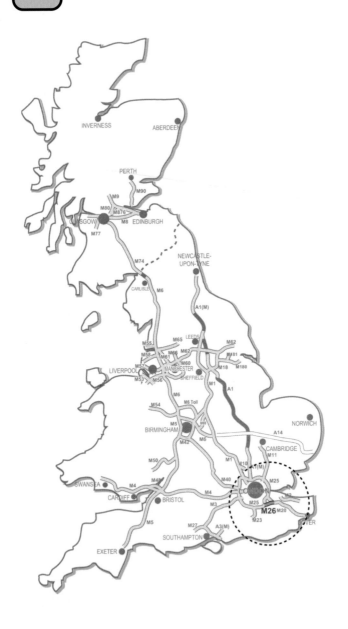

An 8 mile stretch of motorway built in 1980 to form a link from the M20 with the southern segment of the M25. Useful for those who have misread the M20 signs and find themselves on the M26 going west, as they can re-join the M20 at Junction 2a to Wrotham.

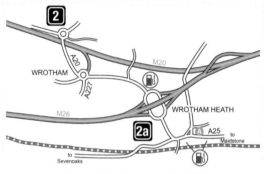

Places of interest
Old Soar Manor NT – 5 miles

 The Vineyard
London Road, Wrotham Heath, Kent
01732 882 330

Satnav
TN15 7RU

Last orders for food: Daily: 2.30pm and 10.00pm.

£££

A family run restaurant, specialising in seafood with French and Italian influences. Although on the road, it is surrounded by a secluded garden and private car park. Small and friendly.

JUNCTIONS 1 TO 12

The M27, 27 miles long, was built to connect Portsmouth and Southampton with the M3. It starts or ends rather abruptly at the edge of the New Forest, but continues as a dual carriageway nearly as far as Bournemouth.

At the Portsmouth end it joins up with the A3(M) before carrying on as a dual- carriageway to Chichester, Brighton and Lewes (with some breaks). It is conceivable that one day there could be a motorway along the south coast to Dover. This would help alleviate the plight of foreign visitors who at present, have to head for London and the M25, whatever their destination.

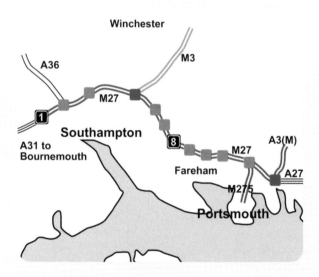

Once off the junction, you might miss the sign to the St. John Barleycorn on your left. To the north of the junction, the road will take you into the New Forest proper, but you will not get lost.

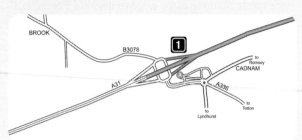

Places of interest
The Rufus Stone – 1 mile
Broadlands House (19th C) Pte – 7 miles

 **Sir John Barleycorn**
Old Romsey Road, Cadnam, Hants.
02380 812 236
www.alcatraz.co.uk

Satnav
SO40 2NP

Last orders for food: Daily: Noon to 9.30pm.

££

The original cottage was the home of the charcoal

burner who discovered the murdered body of King William Rufus in AD1100. It is now a modernised pub cum restaurant owned by the Alcatraz Group. Afternoon teas in the summer.

At the first large roundabout after
the junction take the B3397 to
Hamble. Into the town and bear
right after the church. Then find a
place to park.

Places of interest

The burnt out keel of the Henri
Grace a Dieu at Burseldon but only
at exceptionally low tides.

The Bugle ★

High Street, Hamble le Rice. Hants.
02380 453 000
www.thebuglehamble.co.uk

Satnav
SO31 4HA

Last orders for food: Daily: 2.30pm and 9.30pm.
Sundays: 2.30pm

££

This Grade II listed building has
been restored but retains flagstone floors with exposed
beams and brickwork. A restaurant but the bar will provide simpler fare. The outside seating
overlooks the river and assem-
bled boats.

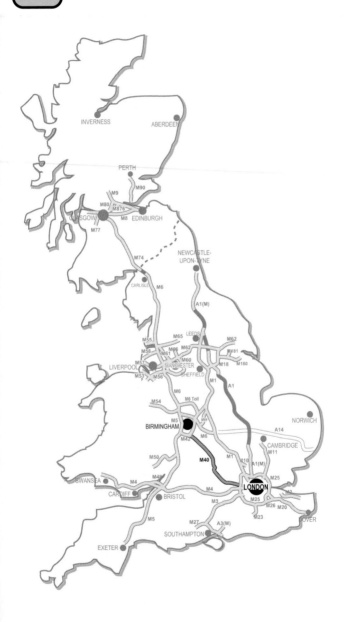

M40 London to Birmingham

JUNCTIONS 1 TO 16

The first section to Oxford was finished in 1976, but it took fifteen years to link it to the M42. It was completed in 1991 to take the pressure off the M1 to such an extent that now it is almost as crowded.

Beware of Junction 15 with five roads converging on the roundabout, as there could be a delay to get to Coventry.

Chesterton Windmill is a prominent landmark on the high ground to the east of the motorway, north of Junction 12. In the nearby church there are original medieval wall paintings.

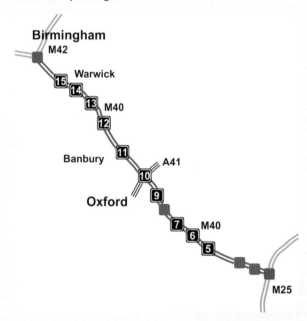

For the Fox and Hounds take the B4012 to Milton Common. After 1 mile turn left to Nettlebed and Christmas Common is 4 miles down the road.

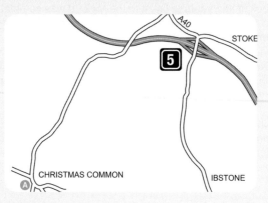

Places of interest
Stonor (12th, 14th & 18th C) HHA – 8 miles
West Wycombe Park (18th C) NT – 7 miles

   # Fox and Hounds
Main Street, Christmas Common, Oxon
01491 612 599
www.thetopfox.co.uk

Satnav
OX49 5HL

Last orders for food: Daily: 2.30pm and 9.30pm.

££

A privately owned classic brick and flint pub with a separate dining room, near the Ridgeway in deep Chilterns countryside. The cooking is styled as modern traditional British and the result is good. They also cater for vegetarians, including vegans.

The road to Lewknor can be easily missed, so look out for the sign on the right. The village itself is attractive. The Half Moon is further on through Watlington. The Sir Charles Napier is to the north of the junction. At Chinnor turn right at the mini roundabout, just after a BP station. Drive for two miles on a narrow lane. The Shepherds Crook in Crowell, on the way, will be friendly if you are too tired to go any further.

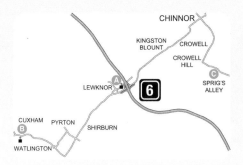

Ⓐ Ye Olde Leather Bottel Satnav OX49 5TW

High Street, Lewknor, Oxon

01844 351 482

Last orders for food: Daily: 2.00pm and 9.30pm. Saturdays and Sundays: 2.30pm and 9.30pm.

£

Ye Olde Leather Bottel is 450 years old and is now a pub with adjoining dining room and bars with age-polished floors. It specialises in home cooking and serves morning coffee as well as Brakspear Traditional Ales. There is plenty of outside seating in a large garden.

Ⓑ **The Half Moon** ★

Main Road, Cuxham, Oxon
01491 614 151
www.thehalf-moon.com

Satnav
OX49 5NF

Last orders for food: Daily: 2.30pm and 9.00pm.
Sundays: Noon to 9.00pm

 £££

A 17th-century thatched country pub complete with low beams, black and red floor tiles, a mix of table and chairs and the resident spaniel. A cheerful family owned place with a mixture of all sorts of people. Excellent menu in the small dining areas but simpler fare can be had at the bar.

Ⓒ **Sir Charles Napier**

Spriggs Alley, Chinnor, Oxon
01494 483 011
www.sircharlesnapier.co.uk

Satnav
OX39 4BX

Last orders for food: Daily: 2.30pm and 9.30pm.
Sundays: 2.30pm.
Closed: Sunday and Monday evenings.

 £££

Situated on the edge of the Chilterns with a large garden and even larger amphorae. In summer you can lunch on the terrace beneath the vines. Very friendly and homely. If you blink you may miss it as it looks from the outside like a cottage on the road.

Coming from London there is no difficulty in exiting, but returning to the motorway you will have to cross over it, take the A40 and (A418) to Oxford and join up with the motorway at Junction 8A. Coming from the north at Junction 8, take the A418 signed Aylesbury and Thame and then the A40 and the A379 to Wallingford.

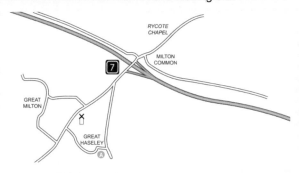

Places of interest
Rycote Chapel (15th C) EH – 1½ miles

The Plough

Rectory Road, Great Haseley, Oxon

Satnav
OX44 7JQ

01844 279 283

Last orders for food: Daily: 2.00pm and 9.30pm. Sundays and Mondays: 2.30pm. No evening meals.

££

A thatch roofed 16th Century pub cum restaurant in the centre of a pleasant rural village. Alison Watkins does the cooking herself and people come from far and near to sample her home made fare which includes bread or ice-cream

Take the Oxford road and after about ½ mile turn off to
the left on the road signposted Weston on the Green.
This will bring you on to the B430 which ends opposite
The Chequers.

The Chequers

Satnav
OX25 3QH

Northampton Road, Weston on the Green, Oxon
01869 351 743
www.chequerswestononthegreen.com

Last orders for food: Daily: 2.00pm and 9.00pm.
Sundays: No evening meals

££

It has had a
makeover, but
still retains a
good atmosphere
with low beams,
dried hops and
flagged floors in
the eating areas.

The Fox and Hounds is on the left in Ardley.

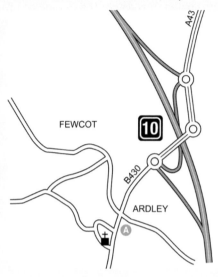

Fox and Hounds

Satnav
OX27 7PE

Main Road, Ardley, Oxon
01869 346 883

Last orders for food: Daily: 2.30pm and 9.00pm.
Sundays: 3.00pm.

££

An old coaching
inn. It now has a
restaurant but
serves bar meals
as well. Helpful
staff who produced
a good soup in
quick order when I
was in a hurry.

From the junction take the A361 towards Daventry. After 1 mile turn right to Chacombe. The George and Dragon is on the left as you come into the village around a bend.

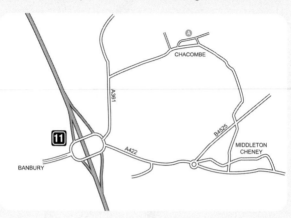

Ⓐ **George and Dragon**

Silver Street, Chacombe, Northants.
01295 711 500
www.georgeanddragonchacombe.com

Satnav
OX17 2JR

Last orders for food: Daily: Noon to 9.30pm.
Sundays: 3.00pm, no evening meals

££

Privately owned it has a reputation for good food. Low

beamed, flag stoned floors with a small restaurant and two dining areas, log fires and a locals bar. The cooking is described as British traditional and they use local meat and vegetables. Some outside seating on a patio when warm enough.

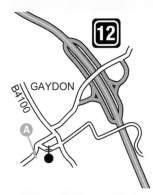

The Malt Shovel is brown signed in the village. The windmill on the hill to the east has long been a landmark. The church in Burton Dassett is an unspoilt medieval example. Compton Verney is one of the great undiscovered art collections of this country.

Places of interest

Compton Verney (18th C) CVH Trust – 4 miles
Heritage Motor Museum – 1 mile
Upton House & Gardens (17th C) NT – 9 miles

 The Malt Shovel Inn
Church Road, Gaydon, Warks.
01926 641 221
www.maltshovelgaydon.co.uk

Satnav
CV35 0ET

Last orders for food: Daily: 2.00pm and 9.00pm.

££

An increasingly popular hostelry with a bar and a restaurant area. The owners who used to run auberges and hotels in France are proud to provide real food, which includes home made meat pies and Real Ale.

Driving north come off at Junction 13. Turn left on the B4100 and then first left on the B4087 to Bishop's Tachbrook. To continue on north; back to the junction, continue over the motorway on the A452 to a roundabout. Left towards the motorway under a bridge and then left at another roundabout and rejoin the M40 at Junction 14. For those driving south it is exactly the same but in reverse!

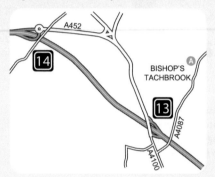

Ⓐ The Leopard ★

Satnav
CV33 9RN

Oakley Wood Road, Bishop's Tachbrook, Warks.
01926 426 466
www.leopardinn.co.uk
Last orders for food: Daily: Noon to 9.00pm.

£££

It has changed hands and also its name reverting to the Leopard. It is an efficient modern hostelry, part of a group of three, with a separate restaurant and a bar for those in more of a hurry.

The junction can get congested, but once on the A429 continue south. Barford is now bypassed – so follow the signs to Barford.

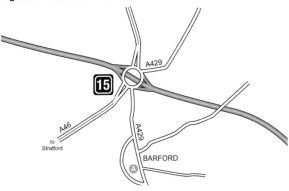

Places of interest
Charlecote Park (1558) NT – 7 miles

The Granville

Wellesbourne Road, Barford, Warks.
01926 624 236
www.granvillebarford.co.uk

Satnav
CV35 8DS

Last orders for food: Daily: 2.30pm and 9.30pm.
Saturdays: Noon to 10.00pm. Sundays: No evening meals.

££

A former coaching inn, now a restaurant with a bar lounge, which has been renovated with a light feminine touch. The food is locally sourced and the young staff are helpful and friendly. A large garden with seating under canopies.

JUNCTIONS **2** TO **14**

Completed in 1986, it might be continued as a motorway to join up with the M1 at Nottingham. It is in effect, the southern and eastern part of the Birmingham Ring Road, with the M6 and the M5 completing the circuit. It is a useful linkage for those using the M40 and also for those who are hoping to avoid the delays at Spaghetti Junction by using the M5.

Beyond Junction 11 it continues as a dual carriageway to link with the M1 at Junction 23A. The church on Breedon on the Hill is a prominent landmark.

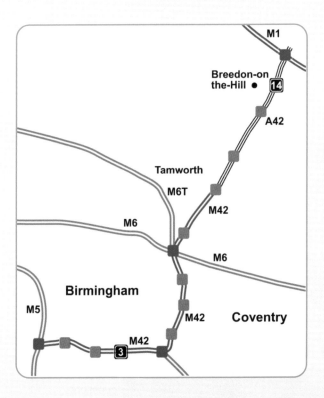

Take the A435 towards Evesham for 1 mile and then the
slip road before the bridge. Return towards the motorway and the Portway is on your left.

Portway Italian Restaurant

Alcester Road, Portway, Warks.
01564 824 794
www.portway.com

Satnav
B48 7HT

Last orders for food: Daily: 2.30pm and
10.00pm. Sundays: No evening meals.
Mondays: Closed.

££

It is a small Italian
restaurant with
good food and
helpful staff. They
were particularly
patient with my
granddaughter's
endless stream of
questions.

Going north, take the road to Castle Donnington. Turn left at the T-junction past Tongue and head into the village. To return you will have to use the A453 to eventually get back onto the M1 at Junction 24. For those going south the reverse applies, but can continue south at Junction 14.

Places of interest

Calke Abbey (1701) NT – 5 miles
Staunton Harold Church (c1655) NT – 5 miles

Ⓐ **The Holly Bush**

Satnav
DE73 8AT

Melbourne Lane, Breedon on the Hill, Derbys.

01332 862 359

www.hollybushinnbreedon.co.uk

Last orders for food: Daily: 2.30pm and 9.30pm.
Sundays: 3.30pm. No evening meals.

££

A 16th Century Tudor inn owned by Janet and Simon Derry with low beamed ceilings, cobbled floors, log fires and a cheerful atmosphere. The food is all cooked in-house and served by friendly staff. They are proud of the bedrooms, but I did not have a chance of trying them out. Dog and children friendly.

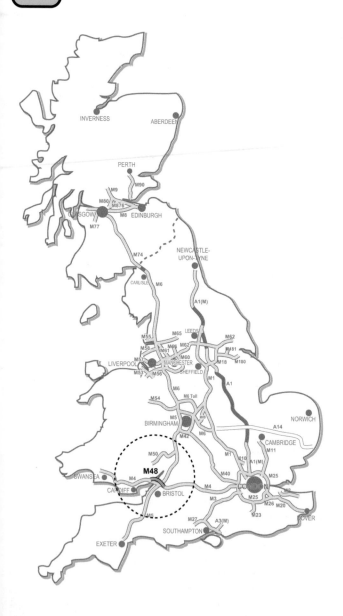

This used to be the last junction on the M4 before crossing over into Wales. With the building of another bridge over the Severn, this section was renamed the M48 and the new section became the M4. The Boars Head is in the village of Aust. For the White Hart take the B4461 towards Thornbury and then left in Elberton to Littleton. Oldbury is cross country via Kington and Cowhill.

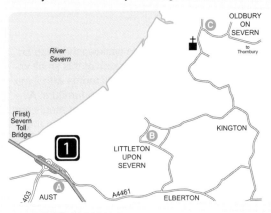

 Boars Head

Main Road, Aust, S. Glos.
01454 632 278
www.marstonstaverns.co.uk

Satnav
BS35 4AX

Last orders for food: Daily: 3.00pm and 9.00pm.
Sundays: No evening meals.

£

A late 18th Century pub which probably was a coaching stop for those crossing over to Wales on the ferry. A friendly welcome to all, enhanced in the winter by log fires and home cooking. There is seating outside where dogs are welcome. Beware the beams.

B The White Hart ★

Satnav **BS35 1NR**

The Village, Littleton-upon-Severn, Glos.
01454 412 275

Last orders for food: Weekdays: 2.00pm and 9.30pm. Saturdays: 2.30pm and 9.30pm. Sundays: 2.30pm and 9.30pm.

 ££

An old whitewashed pub on the outskirts of this small village. Small rooms with a mix of old wooden furniture. A restaurant but bar meals are available. *Petanque* in the garden for *les sportifs*. An interesting Scale and Plat staircase.

C The Anchor Inn ★

Satnav **BS35 1QA**

Church Road, Oldham –on-Severn,Glos.
01454 413 331

Last orders for food: Daily: 2.00pm and 9.30pm. Sundays: 2.30pm and 9.30pm.

 £

A locals pub in this old village by the River Severn. It has the traditional Public Bar and a more comfortable Lounge. A dining area at the rear of the house overlooking the garden.

CHEPSTOW

Castle

R.WYE

A466

YRIC

2

Chepstow is a must for anyone who is motoring nearby. The early Norman Castle resonates power and strength. It used to have a busy shipbuilding business but that has all gone. In its place are many pubs and places along the river.

Places of interest

Tintern Abbey. – 8miles.
Caerwent (Roman Silures) – 5 miles.
Offas Dyke.

 **Afon Gwy Inn** ★

Satnav
NP16 5EZ

Bridge Street, Chepstow, Mon.
01921 620 158
www.afongwy.co.uk

Last orders for food: Daily: 2.00pm and 9.30pm.
Sundays: 2.30pm and 9.30pm.

££

A Grade II listed building of 1735 on the banks of the River Wye which features in Turner's painting of Chepstow. We had an excellent lunch sitting outside in the warm sun looking down on the river. Friendly and helpful owners.

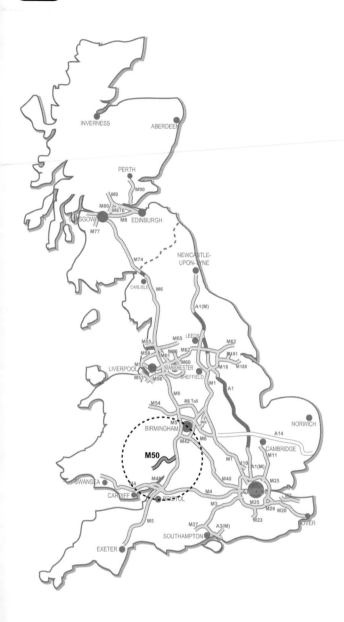

JUNCTIONS **1** TO **4**

The M50 was one of the first motorways to be built and for some years remained in splendid isolation until joined to the M5. It was built to connect the Midlands with South Wales, but only goes as far as Ross on Wye, before continuing as dual-carriageway to Newport. It is also a way of driving to Wales without paying the toll charges levied on the Severn Bridges!

There are plenty of places to see not too far from the motorway. Ross on Wye is a market town with interesting old buildings. Nearby is picturesque Symonds Yat, where the river Wye winds through a gorge below the imposing ruins of Goodrich Castle.

To the south is the Forest of Dean famous, amongst other things, for the small family coal mines still in private ownership.

To the west is the town of Monmouth with its medieval bridge and further on are the ruins of Raglan Castle destroyed by Cromwell.

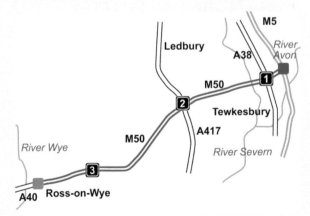

M50 — 1 Malvern / Tewkesbury A38

A relatively easy junction. Just follow the signs to Twyning. The Fleet Inn is brown signed from the roundabout.

Places of interest
Tewkesbury Abbey – 3 miles

A The Fleet Inn

Satnav
GL20 6FL

Fleet Lane, Twyning, Glos.
01684 274 310
www.fleet-inn.co.uk

Last orders for food: Daily: 2.30pm and 9.00pm.
Sundays: No evening meals.

££

By the side of the River Avon, it is a popular pub and restaurant with some bedrooms. An open area for bar meals inside and outside seating on a terrace by the banks of the river. The owner, Mr. Bishop will provide you with his own English wine and sausages.

Take the road to Gloucester to find the Rose and Crown which is about a mile from the junction. Ledbury, to the north, is an attractive market town with a plethora of places to eat; such as the Prince of Wales, Mrs. Muffins Tea Shop, the Malthouse Restaurant and the old coaching inn of The Feathers.

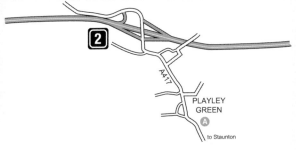

Places of interest
Eastnor Castle (19th C) HHA – 5 miles.

The Rose and Crown

Satnav
GL19 3NB

Main Road, Playley Green, Glos.
01531 650 234
Last orders for food: Daily: 2.30pm and 9.00pm.
Sundays: No evening meals. Mondays: No meals.

£

A simple wayside pub dating from the 1800's, with the addition of a later Assembly Room. Traditional home made food. A party of walkers were resting when last I was there.

The Roadmaker is on the right after 300 yards on the Newent road. For the Yew Tree go on towards Kilcot and turn right on the B4222 then left where signed Clifford Mesne. To get to the Penny Farthing turn left off the junction and first left to Linton. Left again after the church signed Aston Crews.

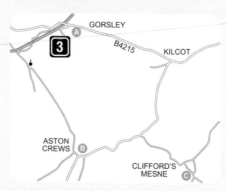

Ⓐ **The Roadmaker Inn**

Satnav **HR9 7SW**

Newent Road, Gorsley, Glos.

01989 720 352

Last orders for food: Daily: 2.30pm and 10.00pm. Sundays: 3.30pm. No evening meals.

 ££

It has changed hands and is now owned by Keschar Sherchan, an ex Ghurka Colour Sergeant. It has been modernised and the service is discreet and friendly. The menu is half English at lunch and wholly Ghurkalese in the evening, which I thoroughly enjoyed.

B **Penny Farthing** ★

Satnav
HR9 7LW

Main Road, Aston Crews.
01989 750 366

Last orders for food: Daily: 2.30pm and 9.00pm.
Sundays: 2.30pm. Mondays: Closed.

££

This pub has appeared in the guide before. It has changed hands and is a welcome break from the journey. Open areas for dining and a bar for quicker meals.

C **The Yew Tree** ★

Satnav
GL18 1JS

May Hill Road, Cliffords Mesne, Glos.
01531 820 719

www.yewtreeinn.com

Last orders for food: Weekdays: 2.30pm and 9.00pm. Sundays: Noon to 4.00pm.
Mondays: Closed. Tuesdays: No lunches

££

It was once a cider house and cider is still a speciality.

The original part dates from the 16th Century so has stone flagged floors and log fires, but the rest is more modern. You can appreciate a distant view of the Malvern Hills from the terrace. Those in need of exercise can climb 971 feet to the top of May Hill.

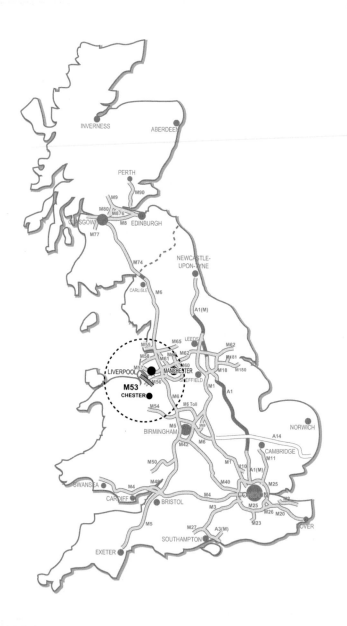

JUNCTIONS 1 TO 12

This short 12 mile stretch of motorway is interesting as it passes through the densely industrialised area of Ellesmere Port as well as some pleasant wooded countryside. Port Sunlight is the home of soap and the Leverhulme house and art collection. There are apparently more millionaires in the Wirral than else-where in the UK excluding the London area!

At the other end of the motorway is Chester, still a walled city with medieval buildings and once the home base of the Roman XX (Victrix) Legion.

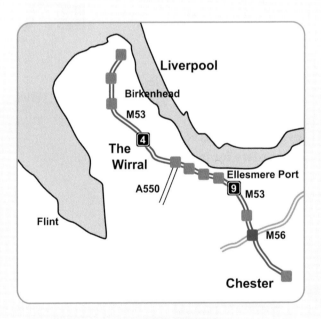

Take the B5137 from the junction towards Heswall. A
mile after Brimstage bear to the right and after another
mile turn right at the T-junction to Barnston. The Fox
and Hounds does not do evening meals but the Ship
nearby (and part of the same group) has 6 bedrooms
and does breakfasts.

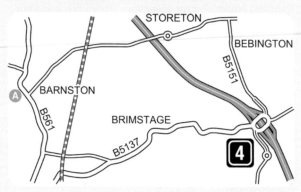

Fox and Hounds ★

Satnav
CH61 1BW

Barnston Road, Barnston, Wirral
0151 648 7685
www.the-fox-hounds.co.uk

Last orders for food: Weekdays: 2.00pm. Sundays: 2.30pm. Lunches only.

   £

Built in 1911 it is a well or-
dered place with a dining
area, a Snug and a large bar
area for bar meals. An eye-
catching collection of 85 brass
ashtrays, 115 horse brasses,
police helmets and 30 flying
ducks will keep you occupied
or diverted whilst ordering.

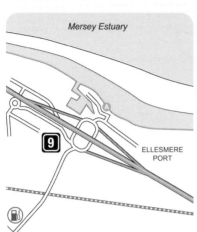

Just follow the signs to the Boat Museum, which is well worth a visit.

Places of interest
The Boat Museum

Ⓐ Jabula Restaurant ★

Satnav
CH65 4FW

South Pier Road, Ellesmere Port, S.Wirral
01513 551 163
www.the-fox-hounds.co.uk
Last orders for food: Daily: 2.30pm and 9.00pm.
Mondays: No lunches.

£

A large airy eating area. It specialises in contemporary South African cooking such as springbok, ostrich or crocodile, served by friendly South African staff.

M54

JUNCTIONS **1** TO **7**

A 23 mile stretch of motorway which was opened in 1975 to link Birmingham to Shrewsbury and Wales. Beyond Telford it has been upgraded to dual- carriageway to the other side of Shrewsbury. After coming off the M6 it passes through pleasant farming countryside until the much vaunted Telford New Town, which is typical of 1960's planning – interminable tree lined roads and round- abouts with sparse signing.

The countryside around is well worth a visit. The Ironbridge Gorge is the cradle of modern industry which is close to medieval Much Wenlock with its Priory. To the west of Telford rises the Wrekin, acting as the gateway to the Welsh Border and close by, the ruins of the Roman administrative town of Viroconium, now Wroxeter, with its massive public baths. Shrewsbury itself is one of the most attractive county towns in England with a wealth of old buildings.

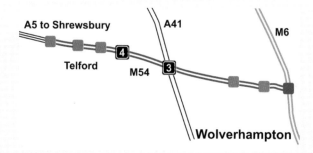

Take the dual carriageway A41 towards Wolverhampton.
After 1.5 miles there is a road bearing right to Albrighton.

(If you miss it there is another one further on.) After the railway bridge there is a road to the right through a housing estate. After a roundabout the grounds of the roses nursery will be evident to the right.

Places of interest
Weston Park (1671) HHA – 4 miles.
Boscobel House (17c) EH – 4 miles.

David Austin Roses

Satnav
WV7 3HB

Bowling Green Lane, Albrighton. Shrops.
01902 376 334
www.davidaustinroses.com

Last orders for food: Daily: 2.30pm, Teas
4.30pm.

££

Many of you will have bought his world famous roses but did you also know that you can have an excellent light lunch while pondering about the future layout of your garden. Even I found myself selecting the odd rose tree to buy.

Get off the M54 at Junction 4 and take the A442 to Bridgnorth, winding around several roundabouts and with endless avenues leading off in different directions. Norton is about 8 miles south.

Places of interest
Ironbridge Gorge

A Hundred House Hotel

Satnav
TF11 9EE

Bridgnorth Road, Norton, Shrops.
01952 730 353
www.hundredhousehotel.co.uk

Last orders for food: Daily: 2.30pm and 9.30pm.
Sundays: Noon to 9.00pm.

£££

Dating back to the 14th Century, it was once a courthouse and the stocks are still in place on the other side of the road. It is now a friendly family hotel with two dining areas and a bar. Good English locally sourced food with a twist using their own home grown herbs.

M56 Manchester to Chester

JUNCTIONS 1 TO 6

Some 37 miles long, it connects Manchester with the commuter areas of Cheshire as well as Chester and North Wales beyond. It is not particularly attractive especially when coming out of Manchester past the Airport. However once over the intersection with the M6 (a complicated junction, badly signed) it gets slightly better. At the end of the motorway it continues into Wales as a dual carriageway.

The historic city of Chester was once the base of the Roman XX (Victrix) Legion. It still has its medieval walls and was where the architect Sir John Vanbrugh grew up.

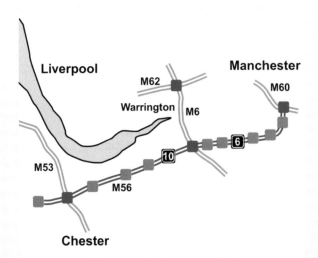

Wilmslow, Macclesfield
Hale A538

From the junction take the A538 towards Wilmslow. After the tunnel underneath the Manchester Airport runway the road rises. The Honey Bee is to your left.

 The Honey Bee ★

Altrincham Road, Morley, Ches.
01625 526 511
www.vintageinn.co.uk/thehoneybeewilmslow

Satnav
SK9 4LT

Last orders for food: Weekdays: Noon to 10.00pm. Sundays: Noon to 9.30pm.

££

It started life privately as Oversley House until about 1950 when it became a residential home for the elderly. It must have been so comfortable that it was then converted into the Oversley House Hotel before assuming its present mantle as a comfortable public house.

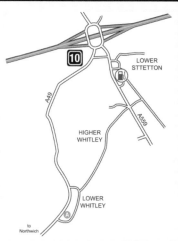

The Chetwode Arms is three miles south on the A49. Take a sharp left beyond the outskirts of Lower Whitley.

Places of interest
Arley Hall (19th C) HHA – 6 miles

 # Chetwode Arms

Street Lane, Lower Whitley, Ches.
01925 730 203
www.chetwodearms.org

Satnav
WA4 4EN

Last orders for food: Daily: 3.00pm and 9.30pm.
Mondays: Closed.

£££

A brick-built former coaching inn. It still exudes the charm and hospitality of a bygone age in the three former bar parlours with open fires. The co-owner is Austrian so from time to time you may be lucky to have *Schnitzel*. Otherwise you will have to be more than content with the high quality of the duck.

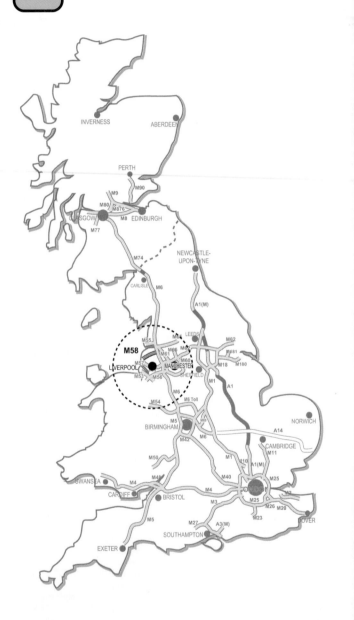

M58

INVERNESS
ABERDEEN
PERTH
M9
M90
M80
M876
M8 EDINBURGH
GLASGOW
M77
M74
NEWCASTLE-UPON-TYNE
CARLISLE
M6
A1(M)
M55
LEEDS
M65
M66
M62
M58
M61
M57
M60
M181
M180
LIVERPOOL
MANCHESTER
M18
M53
M56
SHEFFIELD
M57
M6
M1
A1
M54
M6 Toll
M5
M6
NORWICH
BIRMINGHAM
A14
M42
M6
CAMBRIDGE
M50
M11
M1
M40
A1(M)
M25
SWANSEA
M4
M48
M5
M4
LONDON
M2
CARDIFF
BRISTOL
M4
M25
M26 M20
M3
M23
DOVER
M5
M27
A3(M)
SOUTHAMPTON
EXETER

JUNCTIONS 1 TO 5

Not the most exciting motorway, but it fulfils a useful function of linking Liverpool with the M6 by Wigan. It starts near Aintree Racecourse - the venue for the Grand National. It intersects with the M57 which is the eastern section of a non-existent ring road around Liverpool.

It would be nice to be able to rattle off a list of places to visit off the motorway to reduce the tedium, but that is not possible. The best hope it to look forward to a late lunch or dinner or else to drive into Wigan, long the butt of Music Hall humour but curiously enough, not nearly as bad as its reputation.

Liverpool itself is worth a visit if only to see the Tate of the North in its home in the Docks which is a magnificent example of what can be done with imagination and foresight.

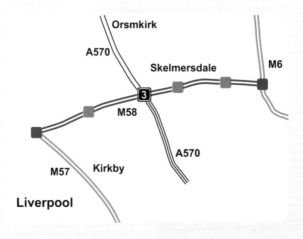

Unless careful you might miss the Quattro Restaurant which is to the left as soon as you get off the roundabout on what looks like a layby.

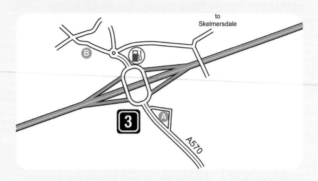

 Quattro

Satnav
L39 0HS

Rainford Road, Bickerstaffe, Lancs.
01695 720 800
www.quattros.co.uk

Last orders for food: Daily: 2.00pm and 9.30pm.
Saturdays: No lunches. Monday: Closed.

                                        £££

As the name implies, it is an Italian restaurant with the usual cheerful atmosphere. It relies on its food rather than beer gardens and the like, to attract customers of which some fifty can lunch or dine at the same time.

The Sandpiper

Satnav
L39 0HD

Ormskirk Road, Bickerstaffe, Lancs.
01695 733 666

Last orders for food: Daily: Noon to 10.00pm.
Sundays: 9.30pm.

£

Once a farmhouse, it is now one of the modern generation purpose designed managed pubs of Mitchell and Butlers with outside seating in a garden. It has a friendly atmosphere and welcome dogs outdoors. Bar meals served all day in an open plan bar area.

JUNCTIONS **1** TO **9**

A useful motorway for those living around Manchester who are going to or coming from the Lake District or the north. It is also an alternative for motorists arriving over the Pennines on the M62 to connect with the M6 going north. Apart from that, there is little that can be said for it.

About the only redeeming feature is the sight of the Pennines to the east looming over the outer suburbs of Manchester and Bolton. The place names in the area, such as Whittle-le-Woods or Bottom o' the' Moor have a certain charm.

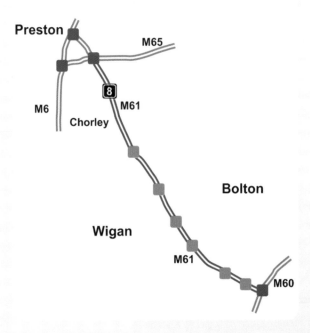

The Red Cat requires concentration as you have to
drive past it and then come round behind it. The
Dressers Arms is further on the right.

Ⓐ **Red Cat**

Blackburn Road, Whittle-le-Woods, Lancs.
01257 263 966
www.theredcat.co.uk

Satnav
PR6 8LL

Last orders for food: Daily: 2.00pm and
10.00pm. Sundays: Noon to 6.00pm.

££

There has been an inn
here since 1805 and is
now a cheerful place,
specialising in modern
British food served in
the flagstoned eating
areas and outside.

The Dressers Arms

Satnav
PR6 8HD

Briers Row, Wheelton, Lancs.
01254 830 041

Last orders for food: Daily: 2.30pm and 9.00pm.

£

A Free House which is reputedly the friendliest pub in Lancashire, with home cooking and Real Ales. It has a dining room and bar serving specialities such as wild boar and venison. Beware the low door on leaving!

JUNCTIONS 1 TO 38

One of the few motorways which run laterally across the country. It is 108 miles long and was completed in 1976 to link the ports of Liverpool and Hull. It does not lend itself to gastronomic feasts.

WESTERN SECTION 6 TO 24

This part, from Liverpool to beyond Manchester, is not pretty. However, once past Junction 21, it climbs up into the Pennines and Junction 22, which at 1221 ft (372m) is the highest point of any motorway in the UK could be a remote spot for picnics near the top. The motorway then descends into the industrial areas of Huddersfield and Bradford.

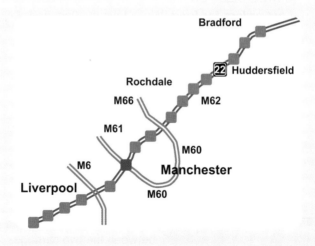

Junction 22 is the highest junction in the country and is
1221 ft or 372 metres above sea level. Take the A 672
towards Riponden. The Turnpike is about three miles on
the left of the road. The views are stunning, marred only
by the street lights along the motorway.

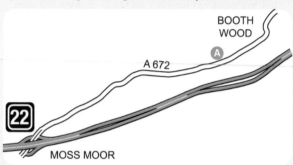

The Turnpike ★

Oldham Road, Rishworth, W.Yorks.
01422 822 789

Satnav
HX6 4QT

Last orders for food: Weekdays: 2.30pm and
9.30pm. Sundays: 3.00pm and 9.00pm.

£

A simple wayside pub, which may have been the
toll for the turnpike road, in the middle of moorland. Faux timber, dimpled plaster, a pin table and

a large TV screen in the
bar area. For the weary
traveller however, there is
a good view over the
reservoir to the Pennines
and an isolated farmhouse
between the two carriage-
ways of the M62.

EASTERN SECTION
JUNCTIONS 25 TO 38

Not the most attractive part of England as it passes through the industrial areas south of Leeds. However, once past the intersection with the A1(M) and the famous Ferrybridge Power Station, the surroundings become more rural, excepting the odd slag heap or power station. It is flat and level and full of drainage ditches and fens.

The M62 crosses over the Ouse at Goole with views over the surrounding countryside. The tower of the Minster at Howden is impressive and the inland port of Goole, made visible by the cranes, is to the south.

The motorway ceases just short of Brough, an old Roman town which was the ferry point for those crossing over the Humber in those days. It continues as a dual carriageway to Hull and the ferry terminals for Rotterdam and Zeebrugge.

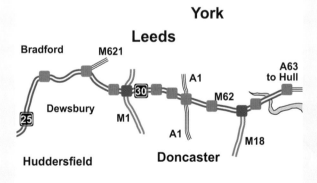

M62 **25** Huddersfield, Feldbrig (A62)
Brighouse, Dewsbury A644

Take the road to Brighouse. After less than half a mile there is a road to the right. Up the hill and bear to the left. The Black Horse is on the left.

 **The Black Horse Inn** ★ Satnav
HD6 4HJ

Towgate, Clifton, W.Yorks.
01484 713 862
www.blackhorseclifton.co.uk

Last orders for food: Weekdays: 2.30pm and
9.30pm. Sundays: 3.00pm and 9.00pm.

£££

Once a 17th century inn it is now a well furnished, friendly family run hostelry. There are two dining rooms and plenty of space with an efficient bar. A well deserved reputation for comfort and ease in this part of the world.

Easy enough to find the Spindle Tree.

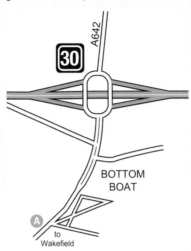

BOTTOM
BOAT

to
Wakefield

 ★ **Spindle Tree**   Satnav
WF3 4AJ

467 Aberford Road, Stanley, S. Yorks.
01924 824 810 (No incoming calls)
www.thespindletree.com

Last orders for food: Daily: 2.00pm and 9.00pm.
Sundays: Noon to 8.00pm.

££

A small wayside pub now
owned by Punch Taverns.
They have refurbished it
with open areas for eating
and a bar. It has a cheerful
and friendly atmosphere.
Outside seating in a gar-
den at the rear.

JUNCTIONS 1 TO 27

For many years the M65 was a short isolated stretch from Blackburn to Colne. It has now been continued to link with the M6 at Preston.

There is not much to say about it except that you are driving through the last remaining vestiges of the Lancashire cotton industry with huge palatial factories of Italianate architecture. The comforting sight of the Pennines visible on both sides of the motorway is welcome.

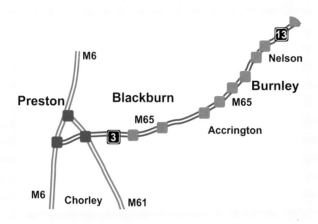

The roundabout at the end of the lead off could be confusing.

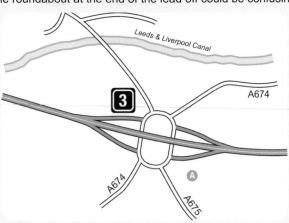

Places of interest
Hoghton Tower (1100-1565) HHA – 3 miles

 Ristorante Alghero

Bolton Road, Withnell, Lancs.
01254 202 222
www.alghero.co.uk

Satnav
PR6 8PB

Last orders for food: Daily: 9.30pm (Dinners only). Sundays: Noon to 9.30pm.

£££

As the name implies, this is a Sardinian restaurant which has a good local reputation and a friendly atmosphere.

As you come off the motorway to Barrowford the Thatch and Thistle is on your left..

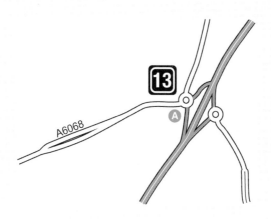

Thatch and Thistle ★

Satnav
BB9 7TZ

Surrey Road, Nelson, Lancs.
01282 615 215

Last orders for food: Daily: Noon to 9.00pm

££

A modern thatched roadhouse which has an American flavour. Large open areas for eating, a pool table for amusement and open (gas) fires for warmth. The welcome is friendly and the staff were very helpful to me.

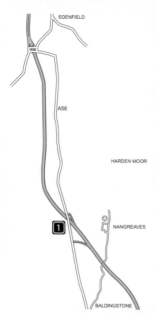

Going north, come off at the junction and left on the A56. After one and half miles turn left at the traffic lights and continue up the hill to Nangreaves. To continue north, drive up the A56 to Edenfield and rejoin there. Coming south you will have to get off at Edenfield before it becomes a motorway and take the A56 south. You can rejoin at Junction 1.

The Lord Raglan

Mount Pleasant, Nr Bury Lancs.
0161 764 6680

Satnav
BL9 6SP

Last orders for food: Daily: 2.00pm and 9.00pm. Sundays: Noon to 8.00pm.

£

It is aptly named Mount Pleasant as you will find yourself on top of the hills in rural Lancashire with a view of moorland and the Pennines. It has been in the same family for three generations so it has a cheerful atmosphere with a friendly staff. The menu will make for a peaceful stopover as well as being refreshed with air.

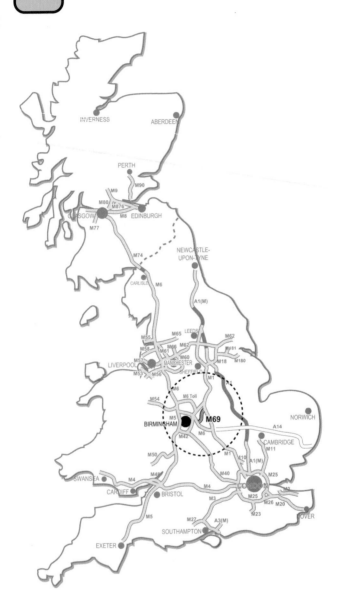

M69 Coventry to Leicester

JUNCTIONS 1 TO

The motorway was built in the mid 1970's to give direct access between Coventry and Leicester. It is comparatively little used so is useful to those who are on the M1 or M40 as a means of driving north or south.

The junction with the M1 is rather abrupt as a result of a decision at the time not to make it into a proper clover leaf exit as the volume of traffic would not warrant the expense.

The building of the motorways has had the curious effect of isolating corners of the countryside to create rural areas of calm, such as the part around Bosworth Field ("...my kingdom for a horse"), which has now been proved to be in the wrong place!

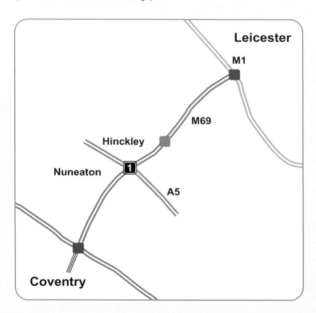

Pretty straight forward for Barnacles Restaurant. For the Blue Pig take the Wolvey Road. In the village there is a modern pub, The Bulls Head to the right and sharp turning just beyond it. Turn right and the Blue Pig is down the road on the left.

Places of interest
Bosworth Battlefield (1485) – 8 miles

A **Barnacles Restaurant** Satnav **LE10 3JA**

Watling Street, N. Hinckley, Warks.
01455 633 220
www.barnaclesrestaurant.co.uk

Last orders for food: Mondays: 9.00pm, no lunches. Tuesdays to Fridays: 2.00pm and 9.00pm. Saturdays: 9.30pm, no lunches. Sundays: 2.30pm, no evening meals.

£££

A privately owned restaurant in pleasant grounds with a lake. It specialises in fish and there is a separately owned fish shop next to the restaurant. Dogs are not welcomed and there are no special facilities for children.

The Blue Pig

Satnav
LE10 3LG

Hall Road, Wolvey, Warks.
01455 220 256

www.thebluepig.co.uk

Last orders for food: Mondays and Tuesdays:
2.00pm and 8.00pm. Wednesdays and Thursdays:
2.00pm and 8.30pm. Fridays and Saturdays:
2.00pm and 9.00pm. Sundays: 2.00pm.

££

An old coaching inn dating from the 15th Century with
exposed masonry walls and low beams with quips such
as "Now Good Digestion wait on Appetite & Health on
Both". There is a restaurant and a bar serving home
cooked specials and Real Ales. It is family run so is
friendly with a good atmosphere. The Sat Nav got me
there with no trouble.

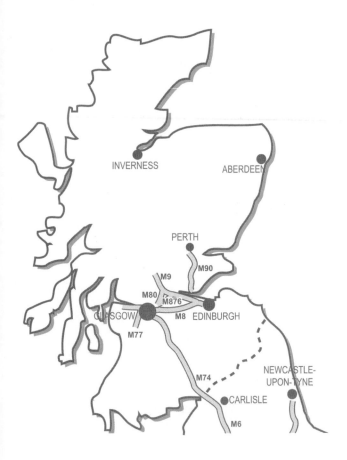

SCOTLAND

Scotland may extend a warm welcome to visitors and even Sassenachs, but for the motorway user you get the impression that the Scots have forgotten the art of hospitality to the passing traveller. Part of this impression may be due to the fact that the new motorways, except for the M74, do not follow the old coaching routes. There are some excellent exceptions to the rule, but there were a lot of places which did not come up to scratch. On the M8 for example, from Edinburgh to Glasgow, there is only one single place worthy of being mentioned, but that is too difficult to find.

The most tedious aspect of the Scottish motorways is the system of linked junctions. It might save money, but it generates unnecessary driving on minor roads.

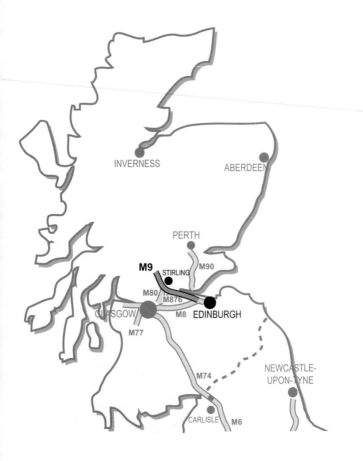

JUNCTIONS **1** TO **11**

Starting near the Airport it passes through agricultural country and past old shale heaps.

You then drive past the impressive ruins of Linlithgow Palace, once one of the great buildings of Europe, admired by the French princesses who were married to Scottish kings. It was burnt in 1745 during the Jacobite Rebellion and has been roofless ever since, but there are rumours that parts could be re-roofed.

The motorway ends north of the equally impressive Stirling Castle, the favourite refuge for the Scottish kings, which was remodelled by James V and is a fine example of Renaissance architecture.

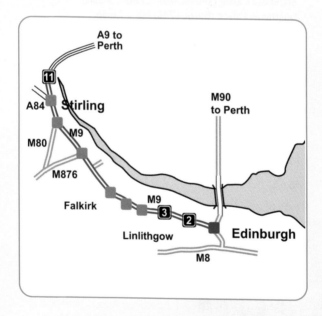

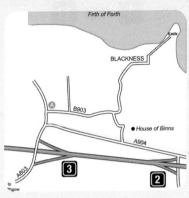

Like most of the junctions these are linked together, depending upon the direction of travel. There are alternative places in Linlithgow to suit most requirements.

Places of interest

Hopetoun House (1699 & 1721) HHA – 4 miles
The House of the Binns (17th C) NTS – 1 miles
Blackness Castle (14th & 16th C) HS – 3 miles
Linlithgow Palace (Burnt 1746) HS – 1 mile

Champany Inn

Champany, W. Lothian
01506 834 532
www.champany.com

Satnav
EH49 7LU

Last orders for food: Daily: 2.00pm and 10.00pm. Saturdays: No lunch in the main restaurant. Sundays: Main restaurant is closed.

       £££

It was once a farmhouse where Mary Queen of Scots

used to come over from Linlithgow to have picnics, hence the name. There is outside seating for hot days as well as a Bistro to suit the more hurried motorist. It is noted for Aberdeen Angus beef and has been named as Meat Restaurant of Great Britain.

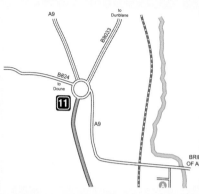

| **11** | Doune B824, Dunblane B8033 Bridge of Allan, Perth A9 | **M9** |

After coming off the roundabout, drive towards the outskirts of the Bridge of Allan. Just before the said bridge, with a high wooded bluff on the other side of the river, turn right. The Inn is to the right.

Places of interest

Doune Castle (14th C) HS – 3 miles
Stirling Castle (13th C & Renaissance) HS – 5 miles
Argyll's Lodging (17th C) HS – 5 miles
The Wallace Monument – 2 miles

Ⓐ **The Old Bridge Inn**

Inverallen Road, Bridge of Allan, Stirlings.
01786 833 335

Satnav
FK9 4JA

Last orders for food: Daily: 2.30pm and 8.45pm.
Mondays: Closed.

££

The Inn was originally surrounded by mills and by Willie's brewery. The interior has been stripped out to make a larger area with rough stone walls and timber panelling to form a comfortable restaurant/bar, where local fish and salmon from the Tay is also served. The thoughtful owners provided me with a newspaper in case I needed an excuse not to converse with my talkative neighbours. The bell from a Glasgow church is used to signal it is time to move on.

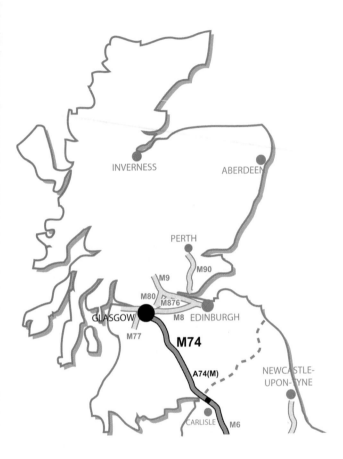

INVERNESS

ABERDEEN

PERTH

M9

M90

M80

M876

GLASGOW

M8 EDINBURGH

M77

M74

A74(M)

NEWCASTLE-UPON-TYNE

CARLISLE M6

JUNCTIONS **4** TO **22**

Within the last few years the A74 has been rebuilt to motorway standards.

North of Junction 13 it is the M74, but south to the Border it is still the A74(M).

Between Scotland and England the section of dual carriageways is being upgraded so there may be delays.

There is nowhere south of Glasgow where you can stop to find a decent meal. However, there are some impressive buildings to see such as Bothwell Castle, Chatelherault, Cadzow Castle and Craigneathen.

The town of Moffat off Junction 15 is interesting and has a variety of places to eat and sleep.

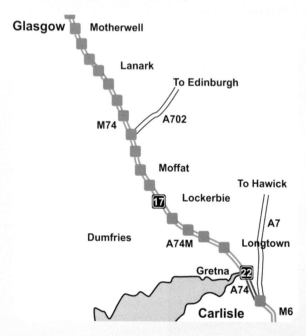

An easy junction. You can see the hotel from the motorway.

B7076

LOCKERBIE

Places of interest
Lochmaben Castle (15thC) HS – 4 miles

 Dryfesdale Hotel

Satnav
DG11 2SF

Nr. Lockerbie, Dumfriesshire
01902 376 334
www.dryfesdalehotel.co.uk

Last orders for food: Daily: 2.00pm and 9.00pm

 £££

The house was built in the late 17th-Century as the Manse and was converted into a hotel in the early 1900's. It has a restaurant and a bar catering for lunches and dinners and bar meals are available for those in a hurry.

This is really for those coming from the south and even then it is a detour to regain the motorway. Those driving down from the north should drive through Gretna Green and follow the B6076.

 **Gretna Green Hotel**

Satnav
DG16 5JB

Sark Bridge, Gretna Green, Dumfriesshire.
01461 337 517

Last orders for food: Daily: 2.30pm and 9.30pm.

£££

It was built in 1865 by the owner of the Toll Bar over the river to house runaway couples. It is still a family run hotel with a comfortable restaurant and bar. There is a secluded and well kept garden. The first (or last) hotel in Scotand.

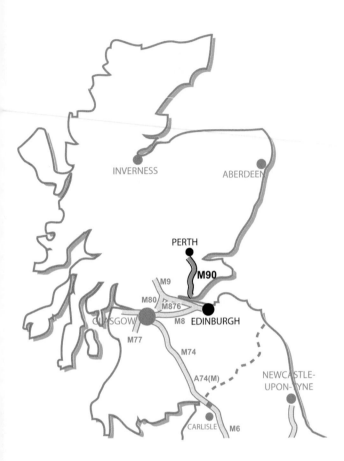

JUNCTIONS 1 TO 11

An interesting motorway which passes Loch Leven, where Mary Queen of Scots was imprisoned and the Lomond Hills are beyond. Further on, the motorway passes Glenfarg and then drops down to the Bridge of Earn. Beyond Moncrieffe Hill are the outskirts of Perth and to the north can be seen the distant outline of the Highlands.

There are castles such as Huntingtower and Elcho to be seen and to the east is Abernethy, where William the Conqueror took the personal submission of the Scottish king Malcolm Canmore in 1072.

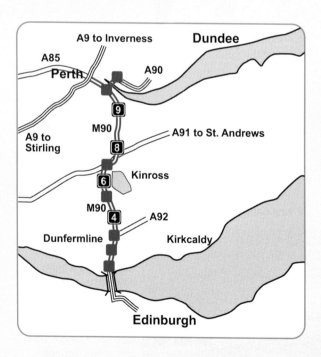

You can see the Baxter from the motorway when coming from the south.

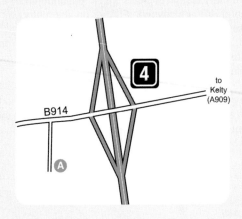

B914

to
Kelty
(A909)

 Baxters

Cocklaw-Mains Farm, Kelty, Fife
01383 832 020
www.baxters.co.uk

Satnav
KY4 0JR

Last orders for food: Daily: Noon to 3.30pm.

££

It was once a farm steading which has been converted and has recently been taken over by the famous Baxters Food Group. It is a light and airy place, where the service is quick and cheerful. A café for those in a hurry and a food shop where Baxters' world famous range of food products can be bought.

The private road to The Grouse and Claret is opposite the Esso Filling Station. If it is full, there are at least four good hotels in Kinross.

Places of interest
Loch Leven Castle (14th C) HS – 2 miles
Kinross House Garden (17th C) HHA – 1 mile

Ⓐ **Grouse and Claret**

Heatheryford, Kinross
01577 864 212
www.grouseandclaret.com

Satnav
KY13 0NQ

Last orders for food: Daily: 2.00pm to 9.00pm.
Sundays: No evening meals. Mondays: Closed.

££

A surprisingly peaceful spot, with a large garden looking onto a small loch. An imaginative menu, combining Scottish ingredients with an Eastern twist, in a comfortable restaurant with a bar.

Those of us who had to endure the twisting road by Glenfarg before the advent of the motorway will remember the Bein Inn. The old road the B996 is still there but access is from Junction 8 or else, at the bottom, at Junction 9.

The Bein Inn ★

Satnav
PH2 9PY

Main Road, Glenfarg, Perthshire
01577 830 216
www.beininn.com

Last orders for food: Daily: Noon to 9.00pm.
Sundays: Noon to 7.00pm.

   ££

Set in a tree covered dip by the old road it was well known to those travelling north or south. It is now family owned and father and son have made it into an efficient well run hotel with a good reputation for food. A cheerful atmosphere made so by the helpful staff.

BRIDGE
OF
EARN

9

A912

to
Abernethy

A913

Ⓐ

to
Gateside

An easy Junction. Take the road to Abernethy. After a mile you will see The Baiglie Inn on the right.

Places of interest

The Round Tower at Abernethy (10th C) – 4 miles

Elcho Castle (16th C) HS – 4 miles

Ⓐ **The Baiglie Inn**

Aberargie, Perth

01738 850 332

www.thebaiglieinn.co.uk

Satnav
PH2 9NF

Last orders for food: Daily: 2.15 and 9.00pm. Saturdays: Noon to 9.00pm. Sundays: Noon to 8.00pm

££

An 1820's coaching inn serving bar meals in a conservatory and traditional fare in the restaurant.

Alphabetical Index

England and Wales

Index by Motorways

Places of Interest Index

A1

-	Shuttleworth Collection	01767 627927
16	Peterborough Cathedral	
17	Elton Hall & Gdns HHA - 3m	01832 280468
45	Bramham Park HHA - 2m	01937 846000
48	Isurium Roman Town - 2m	

A3(M)

2	Stansted Park HHA - 1m	02392 412265

A14

2	Lamport Hall HHA - 4m	01604 686272
	Kelmarsh Hall HHA - 4m	01604 686543
	Cottesbrooke Hall & Gdns HHA - 8m	01604 505808
12	Lyveden New Bield NT - 7m	01832 205358
42	Ickworth House NT - 3m	01284 735720

M1

13	Woburn Abbey HHA - 5m	01525 290333
14	Bletchley Park Pte - 6m	01908 640404
15	Stoke Park Pavillions Pte - 4m	01604 862172
19	Stanford Hall HHA - 2m	01788 860250
29	Hardwick Hall EH - 2m	01246 850430
	Bolsover Castle EH - 1m	01246 822844
	Sutton Scarsdale Hall EH - 1m	01604 735400
	Chatsworth HHA - 18m	01246 582204
	Haddon Hall HHA - 17m	01629 812855
30	Renishaw Hall & Gdns HHA - 3m	01246 432310
	Barlborough Hall Pte - 1m	01246 435138

M3

4A	Napoleon III's Mausoleum, Farnborough Pte - 3m	
5	Old Basing House, Hants C.C. - 5m	01256 467294
6	The Grange EH - 8m	01424 775705

M4

8/9	Dorney Court HHA - 5m	01628 604438
11	Stratfield Saye HHA - 5m	01256 882882

M6

44 Hadrian's Turf Wall

M11

9 Audley End EH - 5m   01799 522842

10 Imperial War Museum - 1m   01223 837267

12 Wimpole Hall NT - 8m   01223 206000

M20

8 Leeds Castle Pte - 2m   01622 765400

    Stoneacre House NT - 3m   01622 862157

M23

10 Wakehurst Place RBG Kew - 6m 01444 894066

M25

4 Lullingstone Castle HHA - 2m   01322 862114

    Lullingstone Roman Villa EH - 2m 01322 863467

6 Chartwell NT - 8m   01732 866368

    Squerryes Court HHA - 7m   01959 562368

    Quebec House NT - 8m   01732 868381

18 Chenies Manor House HHA - 3m 01494 762888

21A St Alban's Abbey Church - 3m

    Verulanium Roman City - 3m   01727 751810

M26

2A Old Soar Manor NT - 5m   01732 811145

    Igtham Mote NT - 6m   01732 810378

M27

1 The Rufus Stone - 1m

    Broadlands Pte - 7m   01794 505010

M40

7 Rycote Chapel EH - 1m

12 Upton House NT - 9m   01295 670266

    Edgehill Battlefield - 4m

15 Charlecote Park NT - 7m   01789 470277

M42

14 The Saxon Church, Breedon on the Hill - 3m

M42

14	Calke Abbey NT - 5m	01332 863822
	Staunton Harold Church NT	01332 863822

M48

2	Chepstow Castle EH	01291 642065
	Tintern Abbey EH - 8m	01291 689251
	Caerwent (Silures Roman Town) - 5m	
	Offa's Dyke	

M50

1	Tewkesbury Abbey - 7m	
2	Eastnor Castle HHA - 5m	01531 633160

M54

3	Weston Park HHA - 4M	01952 852100
	Boscobel House EH - 4m	01902 850244
	Air Museum, Shifnal	01902 376200
	Lilleshall Abbey EH - 11m	01216 256820
4	Ironbridge Gorge	

M56

10	Arley Hall HHA - 6m	01565 777353
	Belmont Hall Pte - 6m	01606 891235

M65

3	Hoghton Tower HHA - 3m	01254 852986

M69

1	Bosworth Battle Field - 8m	

Scotland

M9

2/3	Hopetoun House HHA - 4m	0131 3312451
	The House of Binns NTS - 1m	01506 834255
	Blackness Castle HS - 3m	01506 834807
	Linlithgow Palace HS - 2m	01506 842896
11	Doune Castle HS - 3m	01786 841742
	Stirling Castle HS - 5m	01786 450000

M6

| 11 | Argyll's Lodging HS - 5m | 01786 431316 |

M74

| 17 | Lochmaben Castle HS - 4m | |

M90

6	Loch Leven Castle HS - 2m (by water)	01577 862670
	Kinross House Gdn HHA - 1m	01577 862900
9	Elcho Castle HS - 4m	01738 639998

Reader's Suggestions

If you know of a place which should be included or if there has been a change of ownership which needs an amendment or deletion, then please let us know.

If your suggestion is included in the next edition we will send you a complimentary copy.

Your name and address..
....
....
Telephone...

I would suggest that the following entry be included/amended/deleted.
Name...
Motorway.....Junction.....Village...
....................Details...
....
....
....
....
....
....

By e-mail to **info@cheviot books** or by post to

Cheviot Books
Mill Cottage
Stourton
Warwickshire
CV36 5JA

Reader's Suggestions

If you know of a place which should be included or if there has been a change of ownership which needs an amendment or deletion, then please let us know.

If your suggestion is included in the next edition we will send you a complimentary copy.

Your name and address...
....
....
Telephone..

I would suggest that the following entry be included/amended/deleted.
Name..
Motorway.....Junction.....Village...
....................Details..
....
....
....
....
....
....

By e-mail to **info@cheviot books** or by post to

Cheviot Books
Mill Cottage
Stourton
Warwickshire
CV36 5JA

Reader's Suggestions

If you know of a place which should be included or if there
has been a change of ownership which needs an amendment or deletion, then please let us know.

If your suggestion is included in the next edition we will
send you a complimentary copy.

Your name and address..
....
....
Telephone..

I would suggest that the following entry be included/
amended/deleted.

Name...
Motorway.....Junction.....Village...
....................Details..
....
....
....
....
....
....

By e-mail to **info@cheviot books** or by post to

**Cheviot Books
Mill Cottage
Stourton
Warwickshire
CV36 5JA**